There's No Such Thing as a Sexual Relationship

D1519502

Insurrections: CRITICAL STUDIES IN

RELIGION, POLITICS, AND CULTURE

Insurrections:

CRITICAL STUDIES IN RELIGION, POLITICS, AND CULTURE
Slavoj Žižek, Clayton Crockett, Creston Davis, Jeffrey W. Robbins, Editors

The intersection of religion, politics, and culture is one of the most discussed areas in theory today. It also has the deepest and most wide-ranging impact on the world. Insurrections: Critical Studies in Religion, Politics, and Culture will bring the tools of philosophy and critical theory to the political implications of the religious turn. The series will address a range of religious traditions and political viewpoints in the United States, Europe, and other parts of the world. Without advocating any specific religious or theological stance, the series aims nonetheless to be faithful to the radical emancipatory potential of religion.

For the list of titles in this series, see page 109.

There's No Such Thing as a Sexual Relationship

ALAIN BADIOU *&*
BARBARA CASSIN

Two Lessons on Lacan

Translated by
SUSAN SPITZER *&*
KENNETH REINHARD

Introduction by
KENNETH REINHARD

Columbia University Press   NEW YORK

Columbia University Press
Publishers Since 1893
New York   Chichester, West Sussex
cup.columbia.edu

Il n'y a pas de rapport sexuel. Deux leçons sur "L'Étourdit" de Lacan by Alain Badiou
and Barbara Cassin copyright © 2010 Librairie Arthème Fayard
Copyright © 2017 Columbia University Press
All rights reserved

Library of Congress Cataloging-in-Publication Data
Names: Badiou, Alain, author. | Cassin, Barbara, author.
Title: There's no such thing as a sexual relationship: two lessons on Lacan
    / Alain Badiou and Barbara Cassin; translated by Susan Spitzer and Kenneth
    Reinhard; introduction by Kenneth Reinhard.
Other titles: Il n'y a pas de rapport sexuel. English
Description: New York: Columbia University Press, 2017. | Series: Insurrections:
    critical studies in religion, politics, and culture | Includes bibliographical
    references and index.
Identifiers: LCCN 2016049421 | ISBN 9780231157940 (cloth: alk. paper)
    | ISBN 9780231157957 (pbk.: alk. paper) | ISBN 9780231544429 (e-book)
Subjects: LCSH: Lacan, Jacques, 1901-1981. L'Étourdit. |
    Psychoanalysis—Philosophy.

Columbia University Press books are printed on permanent and durable acid-free
paper.
Printed in the United States of America

Cover & Interior Design: Martin N. Hinze

Contents

Abbreviations of Lacan's Works Cited in the Text

AE   Jacques Lacan, *Autres écrits* (Paris: Seuil, 2001).

  D   Jacques Lacan, *Le séminaire. Livre XVIII, D'un discours qui ne serait pas du semblant* (Paris: Seuil, 2007).

  E   Jacques Lacan, *The Seminar of Jacques Lacan. Book XX, Encore: On Feminine Sexuality, the Limits of Love and Knowledge, 1972–1973,* ed. Jacques-Alain Miller, trans. Bruce Fink (New York: Norton, 1998).

OP   Jacques Lacan, *Le séminaire. Livre XIX, . . . ou pire* (Paris: Seuil, 2011).

OS   Jacques Lacan, *The Seminar of Jacques Lacan. Book XVII, The Other Side of Psychoanalysis,* trans. Russell Grigg (New York: Norton, 2007).

Introduction to Alain Badiou and Barbara Cassin,
There's No Such Thing as a Sexual Relationship:
Two Lessons on Lacan

KENNETH REINHARD

The writings of Jacques Lacan are
notorious for their extreme difficulty, but no text of his has elicited as
much frustration as his 1972 essay "L'Étourdit." When Lacan gave the
piece to Charles Melman for publication in *Scilicet*, the official journal
of Lacan's school at the time, the École Freudienne de Paris, Melman
returned it to him saying it was "an absolutely unreadable, impossible
text . . . no one would ever understand anything in it."[1] "L'Étourdit" was
in fact published in *Scilicet* 4 in 1973 (and republished in 2001 in Lacan's
Autres écrits), but it has retained its reputation as Lacan's most densely
written and intransigent—if not fully unreadable—text. There have been
three impressive (unauthorized) attempts to translate it into English that
I am aware of, but all of them come up against the fact that much of
Lacan's essay consists of more or less untranslatable puns and neologisms,

obscure references, and ambiguous grammar.[2] Melman devoted an entire year of his seminar at the École Freudienne to reading "L'Étourdit," as did Cormac Gallagher at the Irish School for Lacanian Psychoanalysis.[3] The Belgian psychoanalyst Christian Fierens has published almost five hundred pages on "L'Étourdit" (which is itself less than fifty pages long) in two books, *Lecture de l'étourdit* (2002) and *Le discours psychanalytique: une deuxième lecture de L'étourdit de Lacan* (2012). But the question that opens Fierens's first book—"is it readable?"—remains a real problem, beginning with the title itself of Lacan's essay. The French word *étourdi* means something like "scatterbrain" or "absentminded" and Richard Wilbur translated Molière's 1653 play *L'Étourdi* as "The Bungler." The title of Lacan's essay, however, is "L'Étourdit," with a silent final *t*, which is ungrammatical and puzzling for a French reader and lends itself to various homonymic interpretations.[4] Rather than trying to translate the term (which only appears once in Lacan's essay, other than as the title), Susan Spitzer and I have decided to leave it as it is, a proper noun in all its dazzling incomprehensibility.

Lacan dates "L'Étourdit" July 14, 1972, which places it immediately after his 1971–72 seminar . . . *ou pire* and just prior to his famous 1972–73 seminar, *Encore*, in the midst of a remarkably productive late phase of his thinking (roughly from 1968 to 1978), when, as he himself states, he articulated some of his most important ideas, including his theory of the four discourses (Master, University, Hysteric, Analyst), his account of the real as the nonexistence of a sexual *rapport* or relationship, and his formulas of sexuation.[5] "L'Étourdit" can be seen as a condensation or palimpsest of the ideas, diagrams, and linguistic inventions that emerge in these seminars, and there is no question that familiarity with them helps illuminate the navel-like density of the essay.[6]

Both Alain Badiou and Barbara Cassin have long histories of profound engagement with Lacan's thinking. Badiou, who has frequently named Lacan as one of his principle "masters," devoted a year of his seminar (1994–95) to Lacan and antiphilosophy.[7] Already in the late 1960s,

Badiou published two essays in the important Lacanian-Althusserian journal *Cahiers pour l'Analyse*, and a small book (originally a presentation in Althusser's seminar) that involves Lacanian issues, *The Concept of Model*.[8] Badiou's first major book of philosophy, *Theory of the Subject* (1982), includes an extended close reading of Lacan's early essay "Logical Time and the Assertion of Anticipated Certainty" and is composed in the style of a Lacanian seminar. Badiou's great work, *Being and Event* (1988), is framed by references to Lacan and concludes with an important discussion of Lacan and Descartes. And, in Badiou's words, Lacan has a "strategic position" in its sequel, *Logics of Worlds* (2006). Barbara Cassin has written a remarkable book, *Jacques le Sophiste: Lacan, logos et psychanalyse*, since this volume with Badiou appeared, in which she elaborates several of the ideas here and expands her account of Lacan's anti-Aristotelian sophistry. Cassin's most important book to date is the magisterial *L'Effet sophistique*, an extraordinary history and theory of sophistry and its postclassical afterlife, including illuminating discussions of Lacan.[9] Her relationship with Lacan was also personal: in *Jacques le Sophiste* she describes a series of meetings she had with Lacan in the 1970s, at his request, to discuss the concept of doxography—the study of the traces of earlier philosophers' ideas reported by later philosophers, hence touching on the question of the possibility of integral transmission of knowledge, a topic of growing interest to Lacan in the seventies.[10] And even though Badiou and Cassin approach Lacan from quite different perspectives (he as a philosopher, she as a logologist and classicist), they agree that "L'Étourdit" is an exceptionally important and nodal text and key to conceptualizations of their own projects.

***

For Barbara Cassin, Lacan's "L'Étourdit" is "the only text that avoids Aristotelianism, or at any rate the only one among all contemporary texts that gives itself the best chance of avoiding it." In this case, Aristotelianism means the axiomatic construction of logic on the basis of the principle of noncontradiction, which asserts that X and not-X cannot be true of the same thing in the same way at the same time, or, in Aristotle's terms, "the same attribute cannot at the same time belong and not belong to the same subject in the same respect."[20] Cassin demonstrated in her book (written with Michel Narcy), *La Décision du sens*, a translation and commentary on book *Gamma* of Aristotle's *Metaphysics*, that, for Aristotle, before this is the case for things, it is an assumption necessary to language. Language use depends on the stability of words: the individuals in a social group must use words in the same way, with the same intentions—for this is precisely what distinguishes the human being as a rational animal, *zôion logon ekhon*. For Aristotle, this is much more than an academic argument, insofar as he must contend with the disturbing claims of the free-ranging Sophists who blithely ignored and even parodied such linguistic strictures, celebrating language, in Gorgias's expression, as a powerful *pharmakon* that can act as either a poison or a cure (or both), in the hands of a skilled rhetorical practitioner. Aristotle extends this assumption of linguistic consistency into an epistemologically consistent logic that he then projects onto things themselves, which are thereby granted ontological consistency. This is an incontrovertible assertion, as Cassin points out, since to object to it requires the use of speech and thus to participate in a shared linguistic community, which is implicitly based on the belief that words remains stable enough to vouchsafe intersubjective communication. Just as, in Plato's *Republic*, Socrates could not fully refute the Sophist Thrasymachus, but finally was forced to "silence" him by, so to speak, beating him with his own rhetorical stick, so Aristotle combats the threat of sophistry with a kind of sophistic trick (sophistricks?), one that precludes all objections by calling the one who does not accept his "decision of meaning" a "mere plant."[21]

Aristotle and much of the philosophic tradition thereafter assume that a key function of the principle of noncontradiction is the separation of meaning from nonsense (or in Lacan's terms, *sens* from *non-sens*), a distinction the Sophists violated with gleeful abandon. For the Sophists, the line dividing true and false, black and white, was intrinsically blurred, and they discovered in that ambiguity a thousand shades of linguistic gray that could be exploited for rhetorical effect and political intervention, for personal gain or the public weal. But the negation of sense by nonsense depends on and finally reestablishes the primacy of sense; a linguistic act can only seem nonsensical insofar as it functions within a particular logical context, such as the Aristotelian "decision on meaning." Hence Lacan introduces a third category in "L'Étourdit," in excess of the sense/nonsense opposition: *ab-sense*, a term that will be central for both Cassin's and Badiou's readings of the essay.[22] For Cassin, psychoanalysis retrieves and reintroduces a concept of ab-sense that was already implicit in Democritus and other pre-Socratic philosophers, a concept that Aristotle had obscured with the principle of noncontradiction. Lacan's claim that "there's no such thing as a sexual relationship" articulates a principle of ab-sense that is irreducible to the sense/nonsense opposition. If, as Cassin writes, Aristotle's account of meaning is based on an "inside/boundary/ outside" topology, Lacan's logic of ab-sense implies something stranger, perhaps less intuitive, according to Cassin, "a far more complicated, Möbius- and torus-shaped topology."

To return to the formulas of sexuation, which are never far from Cassin's mind here, we might suggest that Aristotle's logic assumes the same closed topology implicit in the logic of man's sexuation: the interiority of the set of "all men" is both established and limited by the claim that there is something external to it, something that would not be a man, namely, a plant. The Möbius strip and the torus are two topological models that Lacan frequently uses in his later seminars to describe the structures of subjectivity, structures that do not operate according to the assumptions about space that orient Euclidean geometry. The Möbius strip violates the recto/verso opposition by having only one side; and the torus warps the inside/outside opposition by having a void in its middle, an "outside" in its "inside," exemplifying what Lacan calls the *extimité* of the subject's relationship to the *objet a*, the bit of exteriority in its most interior and intimate space. The logic of a woman's sexuation will orient the domain of "ab-sense," which has neither a self-identical interiority nor a limiting exteriority. As a principle of neither sense nor nonsense, ab-sense operates according to the intuitionistic logic that proposes that the contradiction of the positive universal (the "not-all," $\overline{\forall x}\,\Phi x$) does *not* imply the existence of a particular negative ($\overline{\exists x}\,\overline{\Phi x}$), as it must according to the propositional form of the principle of noncontradiction. There is no woman who avoids castration, but women cannot be totalized as a set of "all women"; hence *every woman* means something very different from *all men* insofar as what applies to *each* woman (castration) also applies to *every* woman, but not to some hypothetical closed set of *all* women, which does not exist. Against the univocity of meaning that establishes Aristotelian logic and ontology on a well-regulated set of linguistic conventions and the clear distinction between sense and nonsense, Lacan's ab-sense involves a principle of *equivocity* that may seem in comparison like mere "absentmindedness" or *étourdissement*.[23]

Cassin calls the approach to language that embodies this experience of its affective and performative function *logology*, borrowing a term from Novalis, who labeled two parts of his philosophical notebooks from 1798 *Logological Fragments*. In *Jacques le sophiste,* Cassin cites a passage from Novalis's notebooks that expresses her sense of logology:

> Language is such a marvelous and fruitful secret—because when someone speaks merely for the sake of speaking, he utters the most splendid, most original truths. But if he wants to speak about something definite, capricious language makes him say the most ridiculous and confused stuff. This is also the cause of the hatred that so many serious people feel toward language. They notice its mischief, but not the fact that the chattering they scorn is the infinitely serious aspect of language.[26]

For Novalis, philosophy must aspire to logology, which involves the realization that language says something *true* only when one speaks *merely for the sake of speaking*, for the *pleasure* of speaking, rather than to signify something in particular, which leads to misunderstanding and confusion. For Cassin, logology is "the moment when discourse is understood, first of all, in relation to itself and, in more Lacanian terms, language [*la langue*] in relation to *lalangue*";[27] *lalangue* is Lacan's coinage (made by collapsing the article *la* and the noun *langue*, "language" or, more literally, "tongue") and refers to speech as purely sonic chatter, the language the unconscious speaks and hears, speech as rife with jouissance. According to Aristotle, the Sophists "argue for the sake of argument," rather than from any conviction or for any goal, deriving pleasure from something in the sound of their own voices and words,[28] and, for Cassin, it is precisely in these terms that we must read Lacan's "L'Étourdit." Not reading as a process of winnowing away of "nonsense" to get at whatever kernel of "sense" remains, but precisely reading for the *ab-sense* that opens only from refusing to dissimulate the impossibility of the sexual relationship.

***

Alain Badiou's friendly (but profound) disagreement with Barbara Cassin on Lacan's "L'Étourdit" involves, first of all, the question of the status of ambiguity or equivocation in Lacan. For Badiou, Cassin's reading is an especially finely articulated version of the thesis that for Lacan the signifier is irreducibly polyvalent and its interpretation intrinsically interminable—a thesis that we could call, loosely speaking, deconstructive in its resistance to univocal determination. Badiou argues that for Cassin this makes Lacan an enemy of the "univocity of being" as well as meaning and, in this sense, an antiphilosopher (or at least anti-Aristotelian) in his refusal of ontology. For Badiou, however, Lacan's use of "mathemes" and his notion of "formalization" constitute an objection to this account of Lacan's understanding (and practice) of linguistic ambiguity. If Lacan is an antiphilosopher, he is not a "logologist," Badiou argues, insofar as his critique of meaning is not for the sake of championing ambiguity or undecidability, but, on the contrary, is intended to elaborate a mode of knowledge that can be *formalized* and *transmitted without loss*—in a word, knowledge that is *unequivocal*. For Badiou, Lacan's antiphilosophical critique of meaning is in itself a fundamentally philosophical move—for what is philosophy if not the "love of truth," in some distinction from knowledge and its inevitable relativism and perspectivism? Nevertheless, for Badiou, Lacan is an "antiphilosopher" insofar as his attack on meaning is not in the name of truth (which Lacan consistently refers to as a "half-saying," *mi-dire*, intrinsically fragmentary), but a certain kind of "knowledge" *in* (rather than, strictly speaking, "of") *the real*. This knowledge is not ambiguous, since, according to Lacan, it can be transmitted without loss, without the slippages of the signifier that characterize the production of meaning.

Badiou's essay opens by addressing the two senses of *formula* in his title "Formulas of 'L'Étourdit'": first, formula as a knowledge fully transmissible as what Lacan calls his mathemes, the letters, symbols, and diagrams that make up the "formulas of sexuation" that he introduced in the 1970s and that already litter his texts and seminars from the mid-1950s.[29] The other sense of formula in his title, Badiou tells us, involves "a subject's existence" and derives from a line in Rimbaud's prose poem "Vagabonds." In the final passage of the poem, the poet dreams of his brother and strives "to take him back to his primal state as son of the sun" (le rendre à son état primitif de fils du soleil"), for which he seeks an originary ground and "formula": "I, impatient to find the place and the formula" ("moi pressé de trouver le lieu et la formule").[30] In this context, as Badiou indicates, "formula" suggests something like the expression of an unconscious or primal experience of being as well as the subjective affect associated with the urge to rediscover it.[31] In his book *The Century*, Badiou connects this sense of formula in Rimbaud with André Breton's phrase in *Arcanum 17*, "only a magic formula can be effective here," in which Badiou understands formula as a "nominal distillate" of the power of a "creative act." According to Badiou, formula indicates "this slightest point of attachment to the real of that which announces its novelty . . . whereby one word, one word alone, is the same as a body." This act of fusing word and body is exemplary of the art of the twentieth century, which "aimed to conjoin the present, the real intensity of life, and the name of this present as given in the formula" (147). Thus this second sense of formula refers to a *subjective act* of nomination that embodies the immediacy of life itself. So how can these two notions of formula, matheme and act, be thought together? As Badiou writes, "How can a formula be at one and the same time in the register of the matheme and in that of a subject's existence?" And how, Badiou asks, does Lacan move from his well-known elaborations of the vicissitudes of the signifier, the endless phonetic and semantic ambiguities and slippages that characterize the unconscious, to "formulas," understood as unambiguous and completely transmissible, without noise or remainder, *mathemes* that demonstrate that an analytic *act* has taken place?

For Badiou, these questions are bound up with his ongoing investigation of the relationship of psychoanalysis to philosophy. Badiou argues that, like all of the figures he calls "antiphilosophers" (including Kierkegaard, Nietzsche, and Wittgenstein), Lacan tries to *show* philosophy something, an "exceptional object," that it cannot otherwise think, by means of what Cassin calls the apophantic language of analysis. For Lacan, what psychoanalysis shows philosophy is first of all "the real," and in "L'Étourdit," we recall, the real is defined as *ab-sense,* the absence or impossibility of the sexual relationship.[32] Ab-sense as the absence of sense, but not nonsense, which is merely the opposite of sense. In the "formula" that Badiou cites as key to "L'Étourdit," Lacan writes "ab-sense denotes sex . . . *ab-sex sense*" ("l'ab-sens désigne le sexe . . . *sens-absexe*"). "Ab-sex sense" is the formula that emerges from the absence of a sexual relationship, from the fact that sex has no "meaning" beyond itself, that there is no representational distance that would be adequate to it precisely insofar as representation itself is based on draining off of the real of sex, its reduction to phallic signification.

Badiou argues that Lacan's project in "L'Étourdit" is to establish the difference between the discourses of psychoanalysis and philosophy (which operates, according to Lacan, within what he calls the Master's discourse) in order to show philosophy the real that it can't see (the impossibility of a sexual relationship): "L'Étourdit is a disjunctive proposition distinguishing between the discourse of analysis and the discourse of philosophy on the basis of two entirely different ways of constructing the truth/knowledge/real triad, a triad that is in fact . . . common to both discourses." Badiou points out that Lacan's critique is aimed at what he sees as philosophy's attempt to link truth, knowledge, and the real by breaking their essential triplicity and fusing them into pairs: there is knowledge of truth and truth of the real. According to Lacan, philosophy claims that there is a truth adequate to the real, hence that truth is *meaningful;* for psychoanalysis, on the contrary, there is no "truth of the real," which is a *meaningless* formulation. However Lacan argues that there is a kind of psychoanalytic *knowledge* that pertains to or is "in" rather than "of" the real—not "knowledge" in the sense of a particular meaning, but a kind of knowledge whose condition is the *absence of meaning,* the absence of a sexual relationship that constitutes the real. The psychoanalytic critique of philosophy thus is for the sake of demonstrating the *real* of "ab-sex sense" that philosophy cannot accommodate, that exceeds the Aristotelian principle of noncontradiction that divides the world of meaning into "sense" and "nonsense."

According to Badiou, Lacan's critique of philosophy for reducing the relationship of truth, knowledge, and the real into hypostatic pairs amounts to the claim that "the One is." For Badiou, Lacan's frequent statement around the time of "L'Étourdit" that "there is something of (the) One" (*il y a de l'Un*, often compressed as *Yad'lun*) must be taken as a repudiation of the assertion of the being of the One and the oneness of Being, and the difference between these two statements constitutes the crucial point of *decision* that marks the origin of philosophy. As Badiou points out at the very beginning of *Being and Event*, the great ontological decision is between the irreducible multiplicity of being, on the one hand, and the unity of being, on the other. To decide, as Badiou does, for multiplicity is not to dispute that there is a *function* of one; indeed, to "count as one" is a fundamental operation of set theory and a regular procedure of thinking; but to conceive of it this way is "a radical subversion of the speculative, or philosophical, thesis 'the One is.'" According to Badiou, Lacan understands the relationship of truth, knowledge, and the real as a kind of Borromean knot that depends upon the copresence of all three, but is held together only by means of an *act*, the analytic act, which is neither knowledge nor truth but the "demonstration" of the real. The act emerges in the analytic "pass" that marks the conclusion of an analysis, both as the *sign* that something has happened, something has changed in the subjective constellation, and as the *happening* itself, the event of subjective transformation. This is the point of confluence of the matheme and the act, the convergence of the two senses of "formula" in the title of Badiou's essay.

For Badiou, of course, Lacan's claim that philosophy necessarily or invariably decides that the One "is" is not true; philosophy must decide, but its decision is not forced, it can indeed decide against the primacy of the One, as Badiou and other contemporary philosophers do. Lacan's antiphilosophical position does not, however, place him simply outside philosophy; as is the case with all antiphilosophers, Lacan's attempt to demonstrate an exterior to philosophy depends upon the categories of philosophy: ab-sense must be understood as exceeding the dialectic of sense and nonsense; the real can only be the decompletion of the totality of the symbolic and the imaginary. And just as much as antiphilosophy depends upon philosophy, so the philosopher must confront the enigmas and paradoxes presented to it by antiphilosophy, and, first of all, as Badiou insists, it must traverse the antiphilosophy of Lacan.

The essays in this book constitute a moment in an ongoing conversation between Badiou and Cassin, both of whom have much more to say about Lacan elsewhere, in works implicitly or sometimes explicitly addressed to each other. The reader may protest that the absent elephant in the room here is of course Lacan's extraordinary, unreadable, fascinating text itself, "L'Étourdit," which merely in being touched or brushed against emits such sparks of light and heat. Is it translatable? Maybe. Is it readable? Of course! But perhaps only in its ab-sense.

There's No
Such Thing
as a Sexual
Relationship

Authors' Introduction

Of all Lacan's texts, "L'Étourdit," originally published in 1973 in the fourth issue of the journal *Scilicet* and reprinted in 2001 by Éditions du Seuil in the volume *Autres écrits*,[1] is generally considered to be one of his most impenetrable, which is saying a lot when you know its author's long-standing reputation for having a convoluted, gongoristic style.

The reason for this is that "L'Étourdit" brings together many of the most important, but also the most difficult, or paradoxical, aspects of Lacan's thought, taking its definitive form in the early 1970s. It should be recalled that his seminar of the academic year 1972–73, entitled *Encore*,[2] is the one in which the doctrines and formulas that assured Lacan's success can be found in abundance: the theory of the four discourses (the

Master, the Hysteric, the University, and the Analyst), "love makes up for the lack of a sexual relationship," "Woman does not exist," "Language is knowledge's harebrained lucubration about *lalangue*," and so on.

All these topics and a few others as well can be found in highly condensed form in "L'Étourdit." So there is no intention here of providing an exhaustive commentary on the text—or even of adding to the innumerable interpretations that have grown up around it for the past twenty-five years.[3]

Instead, in this short book, we want to propose something completely different: thinking "with" the text, thinking through it, using incisions and extractions, about questions that are close to our hearts. For Barbara Cassin, this means the questions of language and the critique of ontology in their constitutive, sexed relationship with writing. For Alain Badiou, it means the question of the uneasy relationship between psychoanalysis and philosophy. In both cases, as we shall see, a three-term relationship is involved: language, sex, and "fixion," in one case,[4] truth, sex, and knowledge in the other.

What is at stake in these two studies, or readings, or openings, one by a woman and the other by a man (an important point), is indeed knowledge, considered by one of us in terms of its intimate connection with matters of language and by the other in terms of what philosophy purports to say about truth. So, with regard to Lacan's "L'Étourdit," to the modern theory of sexuation, and to the paradoxes of language and the unconscious, the (male) philosopher, at any rate, can say that what we are dealing with here is a new confrontation between, or a new distribution of, the masculinity of Plato and the femininity of sophistics.

Ab-sense, or Lacan from A to D

BARBARA CASSIN

The psychoanalyst is the presence of the sophist in our time, but with a different status.

> —Lacan, *Le Séminaire. Livre XII: Problèmes cruciaux pour la psychanalyse* (Crucial problems for psychoanalysis), session of May 12, 1965

"HIHANAPPÂT"

> —Lacan, *Le Séminaire. Livre XIX: . . . ou pire* (. . . or worse), session of December 15, 1971

Come on, then, and may Heaven bless us with children of whom we shall be the fathers.

> —Molière, *The Blunderer* (*L'Étourdi*), act 5, scene 11)

"L'Étourdit"—a text in French, or even in hyper- or meta-French, that adopts a position on speech, interpretation, and meaning—is, to my mind, the only text that avoids Aristotelianism or, at any rate, the only one among all contemporary texts that gives itself the best chance of avoiding it. This is the case not because it is anti-Aristotelian (which wouldn't make the slightest difference, since, so to speak, a torpedo-boat destroyer is first and foremost a torpedo boat),[1] but because it is adamantly an-Aristotelian, post-Aristotelian, and, to be absolutely precise, ab-Aristotelian. It is the text that escapes, from *On Interpretation* and Book *Gamma* of the *Metaphysics*.

Lacan from A as in Aristotle to D as in Democritus.

A as in Aristotle because Aristotle is Lacan's staple philosophical fare and is also his staple philosophical fare in this philosophically unreadable text, "L'Étourdit."

The first indication of this is that the name Aristotle surrounds the heart of "L'Étourdit," i.e., what the Sphinx says, which is the only passage in quotation marks and the only one in which the word *étourdit*, after its use in the title, appears. Not that I understand the sentences, but the name Aristotle, which crops up everywhere, can be seen just before the riddle of the *notall* (*le pastout*): "Which should be taken not in the sense that, by reducing our quantifiers to Aristotle's reading of them, would make the *existsno* [*nexistun*] equivalent to the *noneis* [*nulnest*] of his universal negative, would bring back the *mē pantes*, the *notall* (which he was nevertheless able to formulate), by testifying to the existence of a subject that says no to the phallic function, and does so by assuming it from the so-called opposition between two particulars" (22; 465).

And the name comes back, shortly after the Pythian Sphinx has expressed her satisfaction—"You have satisfied me, littleman"—when Lacan speaks:

> It pleased me to note that Aristotle failed, oddly enough, to provide us with the terms that I'm borrowing from a different amusement. Wouldn't it have been interesting, though, if he had oriented his World of the *notall* to the point of negating its universality? Existence would thus no longer wither away as a result of particularity, and for Alexander, his master, the warning might have been worthwhile: if it's on account of an ab-sense like-no-other [*comme-pas-un*] by which the universe would be negated that the *notall* that ex-sists slips away, he would have been the very first—a serendipitous term here—to laugh at his plan to "make an empire" of the whole world [*l'univers*].[2]

(25; 469)

Aristotle appears between the universal and laughter here, with a hypothesized ab-sense. Aristotle is Lacan's Other, the Other of the Lacan of "L'Étourdit," who may well drop, in due course, like fly droppings.

D, as in Democritus, since Democritus is the culmination of "L'Étourdit," its grand finale, with the "joke about the *mêden*."[3] Democritus is, roughly speaking, the first/the only one in Antiquity not only to have written the signifier (*mêden*), but to have written it in connection with negation, as Lacan does in "L'Étourdit":

> Were one to *laugh* about it, the language I serve would be telling Democritus' joke about the *mêden* again: doing away with it by dropping the *mê* from (the negation of) the nothing that seems to call it, just as our strip does by itself,[4] to its aid.
>
> Democritus, in effect, gave us the gift of the *atomos,* of the radical real, by eliding the "not," *mê,* from it, but in its subjunctivity, in other words, the modal used for demands requiring the subjunctive to be taken into consideration. As a result of which the *den* was indeed the stowaway, the "clandestine passenger," whose *clam* now controls our destiny.[5]
>
> No more of a materialist in that respect than any sensible person, myself or Marx, for example. But I can't swear that this also holds for Freud: who knows what seed of ecstatic words[6] might have sprung up in his soul from a land where the Kabbala made its way?
>
> (50–51; 494)

So, from Aristotle to Democritus, the Greek knot binding them together is a brutal one, a slipknot in the sense of a noose. If the *den* ends up being a "stowaway," it is because Aristotle forbade it the first-class deck—the open field of "philosophy"—and forced it to go back where it came from, through a radical translation that joins Democritus's operation to physics, meaning, and truth.

Ab-negation, then, by signifier, cut, letter, laughter, anything for the sake of the real: "Democritus laughed (about) everything," *egela panta*, Hyppolytus said: he's the faithful ally of both *l'étourdit* and psychoanalytic interpretation.[7]

* * *

Let's begin with A.

In the December 15, 1971, session of the . . . *ou pire* seminar (thus during the same period as "L'Étourdit"), here is how Lacan spoke about him:

> Read Aristotle's *Metaphysics* and I hope you'll feel, as I do, that it's incredibly stupid[8] . . . Three or four centuries after Aristotle, people naturally began to express the most serious doubts about this text, because they still knew how to read. . . . I must say that Michelet[9] does not hold that opinion and neither do I, because really—how shall I put it—stupidity acts as proof of authenticity, whatever sensible things, so to speak, *i.e.*, whatever is related to the real, may be written. . . . *Aristotle wondered about the principle. Naturally, he didn't have the slightest idea that the principle is this: that there's no such thing as a sexual relationship.*
>
> (*OP* 28–30, my emphasis)

I firmly believe that we are in the middle of a contemporary gigantomachy, to borrow the Platonic term used by Heidegger, here. What is at stake is nothing less than changing the principle of all principles, switching from the principle "there's no such thing as contradiction" to the principle "there's no such thing as a sexual relationship." It is the discursivity of this new principle—"there's no such thing as a sexual relationship"—that "L'Étourdit" puts into play.

To understand both the stakes and the method involved, we need to go back to the principle of noncontradiction as it was established in

Book *Gamma* of the *Metaphysics*—a return to an earlier work of mine on which I must draw.[10] The initial statement of the principle of noncontradiction, may I remind you, is the following: "The same attribute cannot at the same time belong and not belong to the same subject in the same respect." Such a principle is "the most certain of all."[11]

Incredibly stupid.[12]

How is the principle, and the fact that it's stupid, demonstrated?

One cannot demonstrate the principle directly: the principle of all principles cannot be demonstrated directly—that even happens to be the aporia of ultimate foundation, as has been noted from Aristotle *(anankê stênai)* to Heidegger or Karl-Otto Apel. One can only beg (or bugger) the question. But since some poorly educated people keep asking for a demonstration, Aristotle offers them a demonstration by refutation, which implicates *them* insofar as they speak and regardless of what they say. Here is that refutation: "We can, however, demonstrate negatively even that this view is impossible, *if our opponent will only say something*; and if he says nothing, it is absurd to attempt to speak with someone who speaks of nothing, insofar as he does not speak at all. For such a man, as such, is seen already to be *no better than a mere plant*" (*Gamma* 4, 1006a 12–15, my emphasis here and in the following citations [translation modified by the author]).

I'm skipping ahead a bit:

The starting-point for all such arguments is not the demand that our opponent shall say that something either is or is not (for this one might perhaps take to be a begging of the question), but that he shall say something which means something both for himself and for another; for this is necessary, if he really is to say anything. For, if he means nothing, such a man will not be capable of speaking, either with himself or with another. But *if any one grants this, demonstration will be possible*; for we shall already have something definite. *The person responsible for the proof, however, is not he who demonstrates* but he who listens; for while disowning discourse he listens to discourse.

   (*Gamma* 4, 1006a 18–26 [translation modified by the author])

And a few lines later: "If . . . one were to say that the word has an infinite number of meanings, obviously speaking would be impossible; for *not to have one meaning is to have no meaning,* and if words have no meaning, speaking with other people, and indeed with oneself, has been annihilated; for it is impossible to think of anything if we do not think of one thing; but if this *is* possible, one name might be assigned to this thing" (*Gamma* 4, 1006b 6–11).

   What happened? The "pass" happened (*il s'est passe-passé*), that is, Aristotle demonstrated the indemonstrable principle of noncontradiction by means of a series of equivalences, taken as self-evident: to speak is to say something, to say something is to mean something, to mean something is to mean something that has one and only one meaning, the same for oneself and for another person. This is what I have called the "decision of sense."[13] The principle of noncontradiction is established and can only be established this way. It is grounded in the univocity of sense, nothing else, and certainly not in an intuition of the predicate logic type (S cannot be both P and not-P at the same time) or the propositional logic type (if all S are P, then no S is not-P). What is impossible is not for a thing to be the subject of contradictory predicates but for the same word to both have and not have the same meaning at the same time. Meaning is the first thing encountered and able to be encountered that cannot tolerate contradiction. The world is structured like language, and being (*l'étant*) like a meaning.

   The principle established in this way is established in a mean way, because the opponent of the principle will always already have proved its validity by the very fact of speaking. So, when he denies the principle, you can always come back at him with "But you're the one who said it." And he does have to speak, if he's a man, an animal endowed with logos—a man, and not just a plant. Therein lies all the meanness of the refutation, a refutation that's not just pragmatic, time after time (gotcha!), but transcendental, grafted onto the conditions of possibility of language as definitional of man's humanity: speak, if you are a man.[14]

One realizes that the primal opponent of a text such as "L'Étourdit" is Aristotle and that metaphysics, or the science of first principles, is really stupid; if it weren't stupid, I really don't see how "L'Étourdit" could be written. To be able to write it, and for it to be readable (*is* it readable?), the equivalences need to be changed.

Aristotle or ontology as regulation of language	Lacan or psychoanalysis as absentmindedness (*étourdissement*)
There's no such thing as contradiction	There's no such thing as a sexual relationship
Univocity sense=essence	Homonymy and equivocation ab-sense

On the side of philosophy, the sense of a word, contained in its definition, expresses the essence of the thing, and that's why there cannot *not* be univocity: a "man" is a man. On the side of Lacan, the sole sense, the one-sense, is un-sense,[15] that is, the deprived-of-sense (homophony always already enacts equivocation), or rather: it is signification, but not sense.[16] There is no sense other than equivocation, and this is called "ab-sense," an escape from the Aristotelian norm of sense—a norm that is moreover constitutive of the perennial regulation of language, such that it constantly returns, no more or less so than does the unconscious.

"L'Étourdit" is inscribed in homonymy and enacts that homonymy by inscribing it in the letter, that is, by writing it: making of it, right from its title, "L'Étourdit," an enunciation that one can *see*, which is the surest way of hearing it. The schema from *On Interpretation* that goes so far as to include written marks, the *graphomena*, is thus fulfilled, step by step.[17]

It is owing to this twofold operation of equivocation and writing that "L'Étourdit" is situated in the ab-sense that it produces.

The dialogue between the opponents, Aristotle and Lacan, would be as follows:

> ARISTOTLE: You're just a plant.
> LACAN: No, that's what a man is all about.
> But *you're* just an animal.

Here is what I have emphasized (in italics), boiling it down as much as possible:

> *Language* [Lacan's emphasis], then, insofar as this species [*espèce*] has its place therein, has no effect there other than the structure that this impact of the real is caused by. Everything about it [language] that sims [*parest*][18] like a semblance of communication is always a dream, slip of the tongue, or joke.
> *So it's got nothing to do with what's imagined or confirmed in many respects about animal language.*
> The real [in animal language] shouldn't be ruled out as a kind of univocal communication through which animals, too, in serving as models for us, would make us their dolphins [*dauphins*][19]: a function of code, whereby the negative entropy of observation results is produced, operates within it. Moreover, some life behaviors are established therein with symbols that are in every respect similar to ours (the raising of an object to the rank of a signifier of the master [*signifiant du maître*] in the order of the migratory flight, the sym-

bolism of both courtship and threatening displays, work signals, territorial marking), except that these symbols *are never equivocal. These equivocations in which the "aside" of an enunciation is inscribed.*

(47–48; 490–91)

Equivocation is linked to the enunciation ("the fact that one says remains forgotten behind what is said in what is heard"[20]—there's no such thing as animal speech, right? You can't psychoanalyze a dog, or even a cat) and not to the statement of meaning (*l'énoncé du sens*), that is, what Aristotle presents as sense and Lacan reduces to signification. The "symbols" of animal language are never equivocal; those of human language, in the sounds of the voice, and, even more disturbing, in letters (in the letter), are.[21] "We need to distinguish here between the kind of ambiguity that is inscribed by signification—by the loop of the cut—and the suggestion of a hole, that is, of a structure, which makes sense of this ambiguity" (40; 483). The kind of ambiguity that is inscribed by signification is not at all important: the proof is that Aristotle is perfectly able to deal with it. It is necessary and sufficient to disambiguate, and that can always be done by distinguishing between meanings (in Aristotle's sense of the term) and by proposing several words instead of just one: "And it makes no difference even if one were to say a man has several meanings, if only they are limited in number; for to each formula there might be assigned a different word" (*Gamma* 4, 1006a 34-b2). But there is a kind of ambiguity that can't be dealt with, not the kind associated with sense, in Aristotle's sense of the term, that is, with signification in the Lacanian sense, but rather the ambiguity that "makes sense" in the Lacanian sense, because it refers to interpretation and structure. "Interpretation has to do with sense and is contrary to signification" (37; 480). Or again: "The interpretation itself, ambiguous or equivocal so as not to be authoritarian, should make a hole." Or, in plain language for the American students he is addressing: "In no case should a psychoanalytic intervention be academic or directive, that is, authoritarian. *It should be ambiguous.* The analytic

interpretation is not meant to be understood; it is meant to make waves
. . . "[22] He then goes on to speak about "taking a dive into the prompter's
box," "the prompter, of course, being the subject's unconscious."

An act—that's the word for it all right!—duly noted. The Aristotelian landscape of the decision of sense has changed: equivocation has
become the condition or the rule of sense, with a shift in the meaning
of sense.

* * *

And yet, I'm astonished. In no way do those waves erode the description
of the equivocations, in no way do they smooth or wear them away. For
the equivocations are still the ones that Aristotle dealt with, the very same
ones, and they are still classified according to the same three characteristic
levels of the *Organon*: words, sentences, arguments. Here is how they are
described by the Lacan of "L'Étourdit," in three "nodal points" (48; 491).[23]

1. "I'll begin with homophony—on which spelling depends"
(48; 491).

That's only reasonable: spelling is diacritical (which is why "Sarkozy
m'à tuer" ["Sarkozy kiled me"] is so shocking),[24] even if a counterexample
immediately presents itself in French: "les poules couvent au couvent."[25]
This is a homographic challenge to homophony (for a single way of writing the word there are two different ways of pronouncing it, which is the
symmetrical inverse of an "Étourdit," in which the same pronunciation
is valid for the writing of the two different spellings [*étourdi/étourdit*]).
But it is above all *very* philosophically correct—with the psychoanalyst
being in the tradition of the Heideggerian pre-Socratic poet headed
toward language and on the way to *lalangue*:

> The fact that, in this language of mine, as I played on it above, "*deux*"
> ["two"] is a homonym of "*d'eux*" ["of them"], preserves the trace of
> that mind game [*jeu de l'âme*] by which making two-together of

them [*faire d'eux deux-ensemble*] reaches its limit in "making two"
of them [*"faire deux" d'eux*].
Others can be found in this text, from *parêtre* to *s'emblant.* [neolo-
gisms that are pronounced like *paraître* and *semblant*].
I maintain that there are no holds barred when it comes to this, because if anyone is within their range without being able to recognize
where he is, then it is they that make fools of us. Unless the poets
exploit them and the psychoanalyst uses them where appropriate.

(48; 491)

The exact same thing is true, in the Aristotelian homonymy that
constitutes the sole etiology to which all language disorders can be attributed,[26] for the homonymies that *On Sophistical Refutations* classifies
as dependent on language (*para ten lexin*)—hence linked as closely as
possible to the signifier—and which are exemplified in word combination, division, and pronunciation, all of them clearly untranslatable. For
example, depending on whether you aspirate the *o* in the word (*h)oros* or
not, it can mean either "boundary" or "shore"; and if you pronounce *(h)ou
katalueis* like a relative clause it will mean "where you live" (i.e., a house)
whereas if you pronounce it like a negation—"you do not live"—it will
make you say that your house is a negation. As can be seen, the diacritical
power of writing, a handy *pharmakon*,[27] makes it possible to distinguish
between meanings and to eliminate homonymy. The portmanteau- and
palimpsest-type writing of "L'Étourdit" allows it to perform the additional
feat of making the meanings legible as so many ingredients of a mixture
and a pileup, that is, to inscribe the whirling of tropes and the resonance
of what is said in the absentmindedness (*l'étourderie*) of the master whose
"blunders" keep ruining the tricks his valet is knocking himself out playing
for his sake (Mascarille to himself: "And you're compelled to tack and
tack again").[28] This way of keeping homonyms together is similar to the
maneuver of the sophist, who uses homonymy as he pleases because he
goes no further than "what is expressed in the sounds of the voice and

in words" (*Gamma* 5, 1009a 21–2 [translation modified]). Maneuvered
by Aristotle into acting as his opponent (since an Aristotelized person
is someone undergoing Aristotelization), the sophist resists to such an
extent that he ends up getting himself excluded from humanity—he's a
plant, i.e., nature that merely rustles, not even an animal. Yet the sophist's
stratagem is no different from either the poet's or the psychoanalyst's.
Since he is, after all, the first one to enjoy "speaking for its own sake," for
the pleasure of speaking, he could cure the philosopher of his hontology[29]
along the way, provided the latter asks to be cured.

> 2. "For interpretation is backed up here by grammar" (48; 491).

> Thus, the analysts who cling to the guard-rail of "general psychol-
> ogy" aren't even able to see how Freud, in these brilliant cases, is
> making his subjects "recite their lessons" in their own grammar.
> Except that he keeps telling us that, from what each of them says [*du
> dit de chacun*], we must be prepared to revise the "parts of speech"
> we thought we could keep from what they said before.
> This is of course what the linguists set themselves as an ideal, but
> even though the English language sims [*parest*] advantageous to
> Chomsky, I noted that, thanks to an equivocation, my first sentence
> contradicts his transformational tree.[30]
>
> (48–49; 491–92)

In this first sentence written by Lacan on the blackboard, "The fact
that one says remains forgotten behind what is said in what is heard,"[31]
you have the grammatical right to understand: saying (the fact that one
says) remains forgotten "behind what is said in what is heard" and/or to
understand: saying (the fact that one says) remains forgotten "in what is
heard," behind what is said. These are not the same constructions; they
are not the same interpretations. This grammatical equivocation bears the
lovely Greek name *amphibology:* the syntax can be attacked from both

sides at once, as in "*I saw a man being beaten* with my own eyes" and "I saw a man *being beaten with my own eyes*." Or worse: *sigonta legein*, "to speak of silent things," in the neuter accusative plural, and "to speak while keeping silent," in the masculine nominative singular, which combines homophony and amphibology. Make waves (*faites des vagues*). The very ones that *On Sophistical Refutations* diagnoses, disdains, and prohibits.[32]

3. "Number 3 now: it's logic":

> It's logic, without which interpretation would be idiotic, the first people to make use of it, of course, being those who, in order to tran-scendentalize the existence of the unconscious, arm themselves with Freud's remark that the unconscious is indifferent to contradiction. It probably hasn't gotten through to them yet that more than one logic has availed itself of the right to prohibit such a foundation and nonetheless to remain "formalized," meaning suitable for the matheme. Who could blame Freud for such an effect of obscurantism and for the clouds of darkness that, from Jung to Abraham, he promptly gathered in response to him?—Not I, to be sure, who also bear some responsibility on this front [*à cet endroit*] (from my opposite side) [*de mon envers*].[33]
>
> I'd just like to remind you that no logical development, and this has been the case from before Socrates and from elsewhere than in our tradition, has ever derived from anything other than a kernel of paradoxes—to use the universally accepted term by which we designate the equivocations based on this point, which, despite coming third here, could just as well come first or second.
>
> (49; 492)

With "logic," what is involved now, completely in keeping with Aristotle, are certain types of arguments. Aristotle classifies these as falla-cies "independent of language," *exo tês lexeôs*. In effect, they are unrelated to the semantic ambiguity of terms or homonymy, strictly speaking (1 = the first meaning of *logos*, "word," investigated in the *Categories*), or to the grammatical ambiguity of the combination of words in a sentence, or amphibology (2 = the second meaning of *logos*, the "sentence," investigated in *On Interpretation*). Rather, they are related to the combination of sentences, thus to syllogisms themselves (3 = the third, but it could also be considered the first or second meaning of *logos*: "argument," investigated in the *Analytics*). Such arguments, Aristotle further says, are therefore pseudoarguments, either because the argument itself is *formally* false and only apparently conclusive (it is a pseudoargument in the strict sense of the term) or because it is *materially* false, and the premises on which the argument is based already make use of syntactic or semantic homonymies (they are pseudopremises).

It is indeed by dint of logical paradoxes that logic has progressed, ever since the age-old Freudo-Lacanian-type paradox of the liar, that of the Cretan who is reproached for saying he is going to Cracow so that it will be thought he is going to Lemberg when he is really going to Cracow.[34] But not logic only, nor by logic only (besides, what does "logic only" mean?), as soon as you wonder, as an Aristotelian, about what makes it possible to say that "nonbeing *is* nonbeing," that is, about the plurality of meanings of being, which immediately produces paradoxes that no sooner return than they disappear.[35]

Sophistical Refutations in every respect, then, except that—and this is why I am giving long citations—logic, says Lacan, has evolved since Aristotle. There are formal consistencies that are based on principles other than the principle of noncontradiction. In particular, there are some that don't exclude the middle. This doesn't have anything to do with Freud: it is possible to argue, in keeping with Freud, that the unconscious knows no contradiction and to do so completely logically, using a proper matheme, in other words, using a rational (another meaning of *logos*), coherent, and transmissible argument. With the hypothesis of the unconscious, Freud expanded the meaning of sense so as to let nonsense, slips, and dreams back into it. Even if the navel of the dream trembles, what is emphasized by Freud is first and foremost, in accordance with the Aristotelian decision of sense, a "gain in meaning" and coherence, rather than the "fundamental nonsense of all use of sense."[36]

But what about the new logics? Does this mean that these new logics involve a principle of substitution that is not determined by the principle of noncontradiction? They are logics that don't exclude the middle, but did they come up with "There's no such thing as a sexual relationship"? Of course they didn't, even if Lorenzen can help to "unleash" the truth.[37]

So I think we need to make a distinction between two different ways of not being satisfied with Aristotle's principle. First, there is the way that preserves an Aristotelian content, with the decision of sense and coherence determined by contradiction: the age-old notion of "paradox" is based solely on contradiction and disappears along with it, just as both the easily dealt with homonymy of words and the amphibology of sentences do. And Aristotle deals with them constantly. That's where "L'Étourdit" ends.

The other way makes homonymy, amphibology, and paradox the condition of semantic as well as syntactic and syllogistic sense (as opposed to signification). It makes the prompter's box the general or transcendental condition of all sense and logic, hence also the condition of the true-false bivalence that thereby becomes just one particular case. This is a type of equivocation that cannot be dealt with.[38]

This is why I am truly astonished, disappointed even, by the hyper-Aristotelian inventory of equivocations in "L'Étourdit," where it seems to be a point of pride. Because, given the way it is written and all its creativity, "L'Étourdit" ought to leave such an inventory far behind, proceeding otherwise and from elsewhere: from one's conscious consent to the unconscious, which could perhaps be called *Gelassenheit*, or mutual domestication, to which the joke, laughter as interpreter—even as the interpreter of ontology—and as far as can be from the seriousness of Aristotelian logic, should bear witness.

Could it be the case that, by being so far from *Gamma,* we end up being so minutely close to *On Sophistical Refutations*? As though Lacan weren't equal to the primal gigantomachy, duped and seduced as he was by the use of that which dupes and seduces par excellence, the *logos logou kharin* ("speaking for its own sake," "speaking for the pleasure of speaking") of the equivocations that can be easily dealt with. How can we think at one and the same time that Lacan won out against Aristotle (we no longer speak, after "L'Étourdit," in "L'Étourdit," as we did with or in Aristotle; the principle of all principles is no longer the same) and that nothing has changed in terms of the taxonomy that regulates the critical issue of equivocation?

Either (Lacanian) language will already have spoken in Aristotle's logos or Lacan is nothing but an updated Aristotle. Lacan up against Aristotle: if Lacan is a plant, he is not, for someone like Aristotle, a weed to be gotten rid of, but a slightly uprooted plant that can be easily replanted back into the flower bed, that Aristotelian order of discourse whose modular border he constitutes. Lacan in the place of the sophist, able to be dealt with and assimilated Aristotically: "The psychoanalyst is the presence of the sophist in our time, but with a different status": a status that makes him much easier to handle by the order of discourse?[39]

* * *

But let's go on with this hostile exchange, as if it involved two languages that were equally good at comebacks, and see how to highlight the moves.

> ARISTOTLE: You're just a plant.
> LACAN: Oh, go on, you stupid animal!
> A.: Man's an animal endowed
>   with logos.
> L.: Man's a speakingbeing (*parlêtre*).
> A.: *Logos,* I said.
> L.: *Lalangue,* I said.

Each term will be defined again in an ultimately quite univocal way: "We are 'speakingbeings' [*parlêtres*]—a word it would be more advantageous to use than 'unconscious'—because we quibble about idle chatter, for one thing, and over the fact that *it's from language* that we get this crazy idea that there is being."[40] "Write *lalangue* as one word; that's how I'll write it from now on."[41] In other words, as Lacan puts it in "L'Étourdit": "the unconscious, insofar as it is 'structured *like a* language,' namely, *lalangue* that it inhabits, is subject to the ambiguity by which each [language] is distinguished" (47; 490).

All these shifts in terminology are consequences of the primal gigantomachy: "Human beings are afflicted, so to speak, with language. By means of this language they're afflicted with, they compensate for what is an absolutely inescapable fact, namely, that there's no sexual relationship among human beings."[42] The change of language enacts the change of principle and is simultaneously the result of it with regard to two sensitive issues: the letter (writing, inscription) and the relationship to the real.

Lacan sees in Aristotle's *Analytics* "something like a beginning of topology": "It consists precisely in making holes in writing. *All animals are mortal*: you get rid of *animals* and you get rid of *mortals* and in their place you put the ultimate in writing: a simple letter" (*D* 81–82). Aristotle invented writing in letters in logic at the same time as he invented quantification, which is to say that he made a hole in writing with the letter; he made a hole in the universal with the *not-all* that he was able to write. So Lacan may well be the winner the first time around by dominating Aristotle the inventor, precisely insofar as Aristotle was really stupid because he was constrained, restricted by noncontradiction:

This is precisely the basis on which I combine the "all" of the universal—more altered than one might imagine in the *for-all* of the quantifier—with the *there exists a* that the quantic pairs it with, its difference from what's implied by the proposition Aristotle calls "particular" being perfectly obvious. I combine them because the *there exists a* in question, by acting as a limit to the *for-all*, is what affirms or confirms it (an objection that was already raised to Aristotle's contradictory pairs by an old saying).

(15; 459)

So which old saying is it that objects to the universality of noncontradiction? It's just: "The exception proves the rule." No more nor less.[43] The *there exists a* in question acts as a limit to the *for-all*: the exception proves the rule. Really not stupid. Lacan beats Aristotle in that he forces him to confront the structure of the refutative demonstration on which alone the principle of noncontradiction is based. When he formulated the universality of the principle of noncontradiction, Aristotle kept at bay the notion that the other was needed, that the one who not (*celui qui ne pas*) was needed, that there needed to be one for whom not (*un pour qui ne pas*), without which none of this could work. That he needed the sophist as the basis for the principle. Yet it's amazing, and therefore really obvious in the textuality of Book *Gamma,* when the exception—some people who "through want of education" demand a demonstration of the indemonstrable—become "those who seek and love [truth] the most": Empedocles, Democritus, Parmenides, Anaxagoras, and Homer! All of Greece: that's the exception that proves the universal rule (*Gamma* 4, from 1006a 5–11, "some . . . who through want of education," to 5, 1009b 33–9, the gallery of all the founding fathers).

Lacan returns as a sophist, but a sophist who is defined as being necessary to Aristotle's principle, which is to say there is no universal proposition (*l'universelle*) without an exception that founds it; the exception constitutes the universal (*l'universel*). For every man, to speak is to say something, only provided there is at least one man who not (*un homme qui ne pas*).

The fact that everything then comes together/falls apart otherwise is contemporary: a subject, the phallic function, neither true nor false but something fallen in the hole, and a far more complicated Möbius- and torus-shaped topology than the inside/boundary/outside topology that defines Aristotelian sense.[44]

As for the logos, Lacan, with his "like a language," wins another round in the perceptual norm match, namely, the round involving the letter, hundreds of years after the invention of writing. With only the final *t* of "L'Étourdit," he writes and inscribes the letter as primary, as the primary "*dit*-mension."[45]

"I begin with homophony—on which spelling depends," which should be understood as: I begin with inner heterography, culturally audible and internal to homophony. We've moved from the word to the signifier and from the signifier to the letter. Here are a few brief quotations from Lacan to help clarify what is involved. "For the word 'word' I have substituted the word 'signifier,' and this means that it gives rise to equivocation, that is, always to several possible meanings."[46] Switching from "word" to "signifier" would keep us in the realm of easy-to-deal-with equivocation if we were to stick with the signifier, with what we hear. But "the signifier is not the phoneme. *The signifier is the letter. Only the letter makes a hole.*"[47] "There is no letter without some *lalangue*. That's in fact the problem: how can *lalangue* be precipitated into the letter?"[48] And even here in "L'Étourdit": "This saying [of analysis] stems only from the fact that the unconscious, because it is structured *like a* language, namely, the *lalangue* that it inhabits, is subject to the equivocation by which each is distinguished" (47; 491).

For my part, it is "each" that I would immediately like to highlight, an opening onto something that, in Aristotle, is never under any circumstances at work: the differential plurality of languages. "A specific language is nothing but the sum total of the *equivocations that its history has* allowed to remain in it" (47; 490).[49]

If we stop reading here, leaving out the *lalangues* involved and the fact that it's the unconscious that's at issue, in other words, if we take the sentence at face value, what we're doing is composing a dictionary of untranslatables, a vocabulary of European philosophies, which is based on the sum total of the equivocations that the history of each language has allowed to remain in it—the languages of Europe, in this case, since we can't do any better. We draw upon equivocations and homonyms such as *sens* ("direction"), *sens* ("meaning"), and *sens* ("perception"), *mir* ("peace"/"world"/"farming community"), or logos, and we work on them, text by text, like symptoms of worlds.

But there's something more that follows, namely: "A specific language is nothing but the sum total of the equivocations that its history has allowed to remain in it. It is the vein whose real—the only real, as regards the analytic discourse, that brings about its end, the real that there's no such thing as a sexual relationship—has left a deposit in it down through the ages." And here the philosopher may basically become disillusioned or bored. In a dictionary of untranslatables, taking each language as a *lalangue*, one will have found the way in which the real, namely, the fact that there's no such thing as a sexual relationship, has left a deposit. It's not very funny—or *is* it perhaps very funny? Two can play at the game of reduction. But where is the gain in this? The gain lies in going from truth to the real, and the real is that there's no such thing as a sexual relationship, end of story. That's where it all starts from and where it all returns. Being is just one effect of discourse among others, "notably" (*notamment*), and ontology is a shame ("hontology"),[50] but "what can you say"? The real, the fact that there's no such thing as a sexual relationship: no longer notably (*notamment*) but monotably (*monotamment*). The fact that there's no such thing as a sexual relationship. There's no other real and nothing else to be said. It's monotonous. And the way to say it is to write the Real—which, as a result, is not something real—with a capital R. It's easier to write than to say, even though some people may always be nattering on about it.

D'un discours qui ne serait pas du semblant and, later, *Encore* clarify the link between the new principle and the letter. "There's no such thing as a sexual relationship" should obviously not be understood in terms of

hontology: there is no question of essentializing the nonrelationship—
"but people still have sex, don't they?" (*D* 107) Only: "The impossibility
for logic to posit itself in a justifiable way is something quite striking.…
But in this very failure there may be revealed the nature of the proposition that in fact has the closest relationship with language functioning,
namely, the following proposition: the relationship, *the sexual relationship,
cannot be written*" (*D* 135, my emphasis).[51] And:

> Were there no such thing as analytic discourse, you would continue
> to speak like birdbrains [*étourneaux*], to sing the currentdisk-ourse
> [*disque-ourcourant*], making the disk go around, that disk that
> turns because "there's no such thing as a sexual relationship"—a
> formulation that can only be articulated thanks to the entire edifice
> of analytic discourse, and that I have been drumming into you for
> quite some time [from the scatterbrain (*l'étourdi*) to the birdbrain
> (*l'étourneau*) and from the birdbrain to the numbskull (*le serin*),
> aren't they all one family?].
>
> But drumming it into you, I must nevertheless explain it—*it is
> based only on the written in the sense that the sexual relationship
> cannot be written* [my emphasis here]. Everything written stems
> from the fact that it will forever be impossible to write, as such, the
> sexual relationship. It is on that basis that there is a certain effect
> of discourse, which is called writing.
>
> One could, at a pinch, write *x R y,* and say *x* is man, *y* is woman,
> and *R* is the sexual relationship. Why not? The only problem is
> that it's stupid, because what is based on the signifier function [*la
> fonction de signifiant*] of "man" and "woman" are mere signifiers
> that are altogether related to the "curcurrent" [*courcourant*] use of
> language. If there is a discourse that demonstrates that to you, it is
> certainly analytic discourse, because it brings into play the fact that
> woman will never be taken up except *quoad matrem*. Woman serves
> a function in the sexual relationship only qua mother.

Those are overall truths, but they will lead us further. Thanks to what? Thanks to writing.[52]

(*E* 34–35 [translation slightly modified])

When one writes *x R y*, one writes it, but "the only problem is that it's stupid." The woman will never be taken up except *quoad matrem* and the man *quoad castrationem,* meaning: as, *qua, als, hei,* like Aristotle's being (*l'étant*) outside of first philosophy qua number, line, fire, but not qua being.[53] We are in the realm of strict doctrine here, and there's no way out of it: Aristotle "didn't have the slightest idea that the principle is this: that there's no such thing as a sexual relationship" (*OP* 30). "Language, in its function as an existent, in the final analysis only connotes . . . the impossibility of symbolizing the sexual relationship among the beings that . . . inhabit this language, because it is to this habitat that they owe their ability to speak" (*D* 148). If interpreted straightforwardly, this sentence is the final or definitive equivalent of the animal endowed with logos along with—to take the place of the political (man is "more political than any other animal," Aristotle began, precisely because he is endowed with logos)—something of Heidegger's dwelling in its provenance from *die Sprache.*

What difference does it make?

***

In my opinion, there are two kinds of answers to this.

The first answer would be: no, there is nothing purely doctrinal about it, and the proof is that it has to do with the clinic.

That's certainly a good answer overall. It's a way of saying that we're no longer dealing with metaphysics but psychoanalysis—and Lacanian psychoanalysis at that. We? It's up to you to decide whether you're interested in it, whether you're involved in it, or whether you don't care about it, just as it's your rightful right (*droit fil-filant*) not to be interested in Aristotelian metaphysics: there's no such thing as contradiction/no such thing as a sexual relationship, and whether you like it or not, whether you know it or not, that's how you speak, that's how your logos, its logic and logic as such, are underpinned. Take my word for it, your conscious mind is structured like a (generally) logical Aristotelian language. And your unconscious is structured like an ab-sent language, like a *lalangue*. That's how you speak/how it speaks you (*you:* the direct object complement), but so what? Observe the effects, the first of these being the effectiveness of the saying (*dire*) of analysis (how to [really] do things with words)[54]: "The saying of analysis, to the extent that it's effective, produces the apophantic,[55] which, by virtue of its mere ex-sistence, differs from the proposition. This is how it puts the propositional function in its place, since, as I think I've shown, the latter gives us the only prop that makes up for the ab-sense of the sexual relationship" (46–47; 490). Lacan's formulas, like syllogisms in the sphere of sense, are the crutches that allow the analyst, first of all, to get around and be effective in that ab-sense in which you seek his or her help.

The second answer, which is more entertaining for a philosopher who's a connoisseur of Antiquity, involves turning to Democritus, in order to reconnect the two languages.

We're dealing with Lacanian psychoanalysis, at the heart of metaphysical heterodoxy. So we need to begin at the end of "L'Étourdit," basing ourselves on the Democritus who Lacan says gave us the gift of the radical real. It's a philosophically perspicacious way of deontologizing; but how so? Let's read things again and clarify them.

> That won't be progress, since there's none that doesn't bring regret with it, regret about a loss. But were one to *laugh* about it, the language I serve would end up telling Democritus' joke about the *mêden* again: doing away with it by dropping the *mê* from (the negation of) the nothing that seems to call it, as our strip does by itself, to its aid.
>
> Democritus, in effect, gave us the gift of the *atomos*, of the radical real, by eliding the "not," *mê*, from it, but in its subjunctivity, in other words, the modal used for demands requiring the subjunctive

to be taken into consideration. As a result of which the *den* was indeed the stowaway, the clandestine passenger whose *clam* now controls our destiny.

No more of a materialist in that respect than any sensible person, myself or Marx, for example.

(50–51; 494)

For once, I understand everything (I think) about the intertwined strands and the overall *disegno*.

Den is not a Greek word; it isn't in either the Bailly Greek-French dictionary or the Liddell-Scott-Jones Greek-English dictionary, despite the latter's being more complete. It is a word that doesn't exist in the complete lexicon of the Greek language.[56] How can you convey the meaning of a word that doesn't exist in the language? That's what you wonder, too, when you read, and when you translate, Lacan.

Den does, however, appear in an excellent dictionary, the *Dictionnaire étymologique de la langue grecque* by Chantraine, who refers the reader to the Democritus fragment 156, specifically to the formulation *mê mallon to den ê to mêden einai*, where *den* is interpreted as *sôma*, "body," and *mêden* as *kenon*, "void": "to be no more body than void." Chantraine adds that a genitive *denos* can already be found in the Greek lyric poet Alcaeus (700–600 BCE, Alc. 320 LP), "in a doubtful and obscure passage, *kai k'ouden ek denos genoito*, in which *denos* can be translated as 'nothing' or rather 'something.'"[57] "Nothing" or rather "something": now there's a wonderful equivalence for you! And Chantraine concludes: "This has nothing to do with the modern Greek word *den*, meaning 'nothing.'" That's quite a grandiose denial: all theories about *den* are wrong, except for mine![58]

Now for *etymology*, adds Chantraine, since that's what his work as a trailblazer involves: "In Democritus, it [*den*] is clearly a term derived more or less artificially from *ouden*."[59] More or less artificial, and rather more than less, this thing that's not in the dictionaries is something manufactured, made up, a "coined word," as Lacan aptly put it.[60] It is simultaneously a Democritean *terminus technicus* (just as *quiddity* is a scholastic one used to render *to ti ên einai,* which is one of Aristotle's) and a Greek play on words: as if the phrase "were one to *laugh* about it" (*qu'on en* rie) were heard the first time around as coming from the verb "to laugh" (*rire*), while the second time as based on the word "nothing" (*rien*).

To understand the ways in which the word was coined, you need tools such as signifier, writing, negation, modality, one, and, above all, you need the idea of a cut, a false cut. The *den*—if I wanted to define it in such a way that we would still understand the "nothing" in it—is a signifier produced by an atopological cut in the writing of the subjective modal negation, such that, by saying one, the other is also produced. Indeed, all of this is inscribed in the *den*.

Let's begin again with the Democritus fragment DK 156B, with a bit of basic philology now. A pre-Socratic fragment, such as this one, is listed in the original sourcebook, the bible that is the Diels edition as revised by Kranz (whence the initials DK): *Die Fragmente der Vorsokratiker.*[61] The fact that it is listed as a "B-fragment" means that it is regarded as an "authentic" fragment, as opposed to the testimonia, which are referred to as "A-fragments." It is authentic, but in a heterogeneous context, in this instance a text by Plutarch, *Against Colotes* (4, 1108F), that cites it, a text written six hundred years after Democritus as a response to one of Epicurus's disciples. So the meaning of its meaning is not self-evident. I would simply say that Plutarch, flirting with his opponent, albeit in a properly philosophical way, was trying to get Democritus back on the right side of metaphysics by separating him (rightly so, of course, in Lacan's opinion as well as my own) from Protagoras and the sophistic confusion to which Colotes had assimilated him. He thus gives the fragment (in italics), followed by its intralinguistic translation into the language of metaphysics:

Ho Kolôtês esphalê peri lexin tou andros, en hêi diorizetai mê mallon
to den ê to mêden einai, *den men onomazôn to sôma, mêden de to
kenon, hôs kai toutou phusin tina kai hupostasin idian tou ekhontos.*

Colotes misunderstood the way our man spoke when he makes the
following distinction: *the* den *no more exists than the* mêden; Democritus means "body" by "*den*" and "void" by "*mêden*," indicating
that the latter, too, has a certain nature and subsistence of its own.[62]

The "reality" of this fragment and of the invention of the *den* is also
attested by two other testimonia (hence A-fragments), one by Galen (a
century after Plutarch) and the other by Simplicius (another three centu-
ries after Galen). These are extremely interesting texts, each with its own
thematics and systematics, written in a fairly pure philosophical language.
In short, when you read them, the passion for doxography, linked to field
research on transmission, interpretation, distortion, reconstruction, and
failure—the pass?[63]—might grab you the way it has me.[64]

    To deal with *On the Elements According to Hippocrates,* Galen, the
doctor, proceeded by way of an analysis of Democritus and, more precisely,
by way of an analysis of the ways in which Democritus distinguished
linguistic convention (*nomôi*, "by convention," "according to the law")
from something like the real (making use of a very unusual term here:
eteêi, "in reality," as it is usually translated, or "genuinely," from *eteos*,
"true, genuine"): "by convention sweet and by convention bitter ... by
convention color; but in reality atoms and void,' said Democritus."[65]
Galen then proposed an interpretation and intralinguistic translation
of this strange Democritean terminology: "The expression 'by convention' means exactly this: 'by custom' [*nomisti*], as it were, and 'relative
to us,' not in accordance with the actual nature of things [*kat' autôn tôn
pragmatôn tên phusin*]; he speaks of the latter, in turn, of 'in reality,'
taking the word from the term 'real,' which means 'true.' And the whole
meaning of his statement would be this: Among men something is held
to be white and black and sweet and bitter and all else of this kind, but

in truth the totality of things is *den* and *mêden* [*kata de tên alêtheian den kai mêden esti ta panta*]."

When he reaches these words, Galen can only continue his explanation by changing the language he uses: "For he himself [Democritus] said this too when he called the atoms *den* and the void *mêden*."⁶⁶ So we have *den*: body and atoms (soon to be defined as little bodies, *khôris*, separated from one another) and *mêden*: the void (*to kenon*, soon to be defined as *khôra*, but let's leave that aside . . .).

Simplicius the Aristotelian, commenting on Aristotle's *On the Heavens,* concluded with a definite, even definitive, interpretation: "Democritus thinks that the nature of eternal things consists in small substances, infinite in quantity [*mikras ousias plêthos apeirous*], and for them he posits a place, distinct from them and infinite in extent. He calls [this] place by the names 'void' [*to kenôi*], 'nothing' [*toi oudeni*], and 'infinite'; and each of the substances he calls '*den*,' 'solid' [*tôi nastoi*], and 'being' [*tôi onti*]."⁶⁷

Move along, there's nothing to see here. *Den* is being (*l'étant*). Aristotle and ontology have won. Democritus amounts to the same, and the real is only ever something true and natural.

Let's start over again with the word that doesn't exist, because *it* doesn't deceive. It doesn't exist in a very specific way. Like all signs, it is "arbitrary," in the sense that its only value lies in being different. What *does* exist, and which it is different from, is the negative term, which can take two forms, *ouden* or *mêden*. These are two adjectives ("no" in the masculine and feminine forms) and two pronouns ("no one," "nothing"), which, in the neuter accusative, can act as adverbs ("in no way," "not at all"). The fact that there are two of them is very characteristic of the Greek language: it has two types of negation, a so-called factual, or objective, negation, in *ou*, and a modal negation, of impossibility and prohibition, a so-called prohibitive, subjective negation, in *mê*. The latter is used, primarily in moods other than the indicative, in both main and subordinate clauses, for orders, warnings, wishes and regrets, and eventualities and possibilities that are denied or feared. *Mêden,* like *mê on*, is something that cannot and must not be, or "be there" or "be such and such a way"; it is nothingness, perhaps. *Ouden*, on the other hand, like *ouk on*, is merely something that is not, that is not there, that is not such and such a way, but might well be or might have been: a person who is dead, for example, or "something not there" (*un rien*), perhaps.[68] So *den* contrasts with *ouden* (Simplicius) and, in a more insistent, assertive way, with *mêden* (Plutarch, Galen).

In both cases, the negative word is very obvious: it is based on *hen*, "one," the numerical adjective in the neuter, preceded by a negative prefix. What's more, it is not a question of simple negation (*ou* or *mê*: "not"), but of the simplest of compound negatives, compounded, in this case, with the commonest and smallest negative prefix in Greek: *de* (*ou-de, mê-de*: "not even," like the Latin *ne quidem*, or "neither . . . nor" when it is doubled).[69] So in *ouden*, as in *mêden*, one hears: *oude hen*, "not even one," and in *mêde hen* "not even, and especially not, one." From *oude hen* and *mêde hen* to *ouden* and *mêden*, it follows inexorably: this is proper Greek, sound etymology.

The problem is that, along this road, you don't encounter *den*. I would even say that it is impossible to encounter *den* when you follow the thread of language (and to say that sentence in Greek I would use *mê*, not *ou*!). *Den* is the product of a false cut, anomalous when compared with the etymology inscribed in words: it is something of a signed signifier, a deliberate fabrication, the mark of a difference.

Affirmation	Objective negation	Subjective negation	Signifying invention
Hen	*Ouden* =*oud'hen*	*Meden* =*med'hen*	*me/den* → *Den*
(root word)	(etymology)	(etymology)	(false cut)
"one"	"nothing" =not even one	"nothing" =anything but one	less than nothing

I would add that it is impossible to regard this as anything but a sort of violence, a violence that would be evident, I dare say, to all Greeks. I call Homer and Plato as my witnesses.

Plato first, since he testifies about the immediate perception of the etymon in *mêden*. Thus, in *The Sophist,* the Stranger (with parricide on the horizon) shows how, if you stick to Parmenides and his statement "nonbeing is not," the very possibility of falsity disappears since, in one way or another, falsity causes what-is-not to *be*. Fortunately, Parmenides' logos itself, his statement as he states it, his enunciation, therefore, if it is tortured a bit, admits that nonbeing is. Parmenides says in effect: "Never can things that are not—*mê onta*—be forced to be."[70] However, this is doubly contradictory, both because the logos confers a certain kind of existence on nonbeings merely by saying them (words are not nothing) and because it is a plural ("nonbeings," "things that are not"), and quantity is obviously quantity *of* something, of a unit, or, in other words, the plural only exists in relation to the singular.

> THE STRANGER: Do you consent to this point and consider that it's a necessity for him who is saying something [*ti*] to say at least some one thing [*hen ge ti*]?
>
> THEAETETUS: That's so.
>
> THE STRANGER: For you'll assert that at least "something" [*ti*] is a sign of one [*hen*], and "a pair of somethings" [*tine*] of two, and "somethings" [*tines*] of many.
>
> THEAETETUS: Of course.
>
> THE STRANGER: It does seem, then, that it's most necessary for him who is not saying something [*mê ti*] to be saying, absolutely, as it seems, nothing [*mêden*].[71]

Hen ti, mê ti, mêden, an insistence on number: nothing is "not even one," *mêd'hen*, and this is heard to such an extent that it serves as a matrix for the demonstrative evidence. Saying *mêden* becomes a performative self-contradiction.

And it's against the backdrop of Homer as the great precursor, as usual. It is indeed the quintessential wordplay of the *Odyssey* that resonates beneath it, and Bérard speaks affably of an "avalanche of puns."[72] We are with Odysseus and his companions in the cave of the Cyclops. Instead of welcoming them as their host, the monster devours two of them for dinner, washing them down with milk from his sheep. The next day he goes out to graze his flock. When he returns, after milking the sheep, he gobbles up another two of Odysseus's companions. Odysseus, who has had time to think it all over and hatch his plot, offers him a big bowl of wine. The Cyclops asks for three refills and winds up getting drunk to the gills. Odysseus then says, "So you ask me the name I'm known by, Cyclops? . . . Nobody [*Outis*]—that's my name. Nobody [*Outis*]—so my mother and father call me, all my friends call me" (9.408–11).[73]

The drunkard falls asleep. Odysseus and his companions blind him with a red-hot stake made from an olive branch. Polyphemus wrenches the bloody stake out of his eye and bellows to rouse his neighbors. The other Cyclopes cry out to him: "Is somebody [*mê tis*] rustling your flocks against your will?" "Is somebody [*mê tis*] trying to kill you now by fraud or force?" Is somebody . . . ?—*mê tis,* because they do not believe there can actually *be* somebody: To which the Cyclops can only reply, "*Nobody*, friends, is killing me now, by fraud and not by force!", *Outis me kteinei* (9.454).[74] The same sentence is construed to mean "Nobody's killing me now, by fraud and not by force" by Polyphemus who says it and "Nobody's killing me now either by fraud or by force" by the Cyclopes who hear it. And it is here that we can gauge all the usefulness of the pleonastic *ne* in French, which Lacan, moreover, armed with Damourette and Pichon,[75] always made a big deal about:[76] Polyphemus, in proper French, would have made himself understood or he would have been corrected. And the chorus of Cyclopes continues: "If you're alone . . . and nobody's [*mê tis*] trying to overpower you now—look, it must be a plague sent here by mighty Zeus and there's no escape from *that*. You'd better pray to your father, Lord Poseidon." The Cyclopes lumber off and Odysseus is then heard in voice-over: "laughter filled my heart to think how my name had duped them one and all, and my great *mêtis*" (that is, my cunning and my plan) (9.461–63 [translation modified by the author]).[77]

From *Outis*, a proper noun denoting a person, hence someone, to *outis*, a negation in a sentence, "no one," in the sense of *ou . . . tis*, "not someone," "nobody." Then, from *Outis* and *ou . . . tis* to *mê . . . tis* and *mêtis*, the signifying chain is in place right from the start in Odysseus's mind. This is even precisely what the term *mêtis* denotes: intelligence—from the overall perspective and Zeus's great plan to the cunning of Odysseus's tricks—intelligence, of either the naturally technical or the artistic variety, both that of the octopus and that of the sophist, including the intelligence involved in that skill peculiar to human beings, linguistic skill. Odysseus's *mêtis* uses logos in its grammatical and syntactic operations, where it connects with semantics proper, to wit: where equivocation comes into play. Just think about what happens when a cocky Odysseus (out of narcissism or out of his quest for identity?) emerges from the efficiency of wordplay to shout from his departing ship who he is to the Cyclops, who is still within hearing range: "Cyclops—if any man on the face of the earth should ask you who blinded you, shamed you so—say Odysseus, raider of cities, *he* gouged out your eye, Laertes' son who makes his home in Ithaca!" (9.558–62). Polyphemus implores Poseidon to cast a great curse on him. The Greeks were so close to their goal, and now, on account of these needless remarks, they are back to square one.

Homer serves as a witness for me here, first and foremost as regards the force of etymology, since it makes linguistic decomposition ever imminent: *ou/mê tis*, not somebody, anything but somebody, nobody.

But the *mêtis* of Homer's language, in its first calm yet disruptive wordplay, also bears witness to the positive/negative two-sidedness and the ease of reversal. Negation has an ontologically charged heredity; standard French, to an even greater extent than Greek, testifies to this. Thus, "nobody" (*personne*) was originally somebody, a person (*une personne*), from *persona*, the actor's mask, which is hardly something insignificant. And "nothing" (*rien*) was originally *rem*, a thing, in the accusative, *une rien* (feminine) in Old French, which *un rien* (masculine) gradually did away with: "The word," as the *Dictionnaire historique de la langue française* in fact says, "provides an abridged version of the evolution of the etymological meaning of 'thing' reversed into 'nothingness.'" The same is true of the Spanish *nada*, based on the Latin (*res*) *nata* (the past participle of *nasci*, "to be born"), "nothing": "something born." And when it's not the positive thing that changes meaning directly, the difference between, and creativity of, languages can be seen in the choice of what is negated, for example: "I don't believe it," "I can't see a thing," "I don't understand jack about it," and even "I don't understand diddly squat about it."[78] *Mêden, mêtis,* not one, not anyone; *nihil*: no *hilum* (if the dictionaries know what they're talking about), that little black spot at one end of a bean, and *nemo*, not a man; "nothing" and "nobody," not a thing and not a body; and *nichts* ("nothing" in German), not a *Wiht*, a little demon, in terms of *muthos*, or, in terms of *logos*, not a *Wicht*, from *Wesen*, "essence."

It is from this general order of languages, the order of their meaning, that the *den* differs even as it reveals it. Through the odd conflation of the last letter of the negation and the negated positive, it forces us to understand that the atom is not only not an affirmation or a position—being or the one—but that it is also not their negation, that it does not have the consistency of "no-thingness" or of "nothing." The atom is literally less than nothing; it should be called "othing" (*ien*) or, to preserve its rejected etymology, "ot-one" (*iun*).[79] *Den, ot-one* is the name of the atom insofar as it can no longer be confused with the being of ontology or be regarded as an elementary body in physics.

German, in particular the German of the Diels-Kranz translation, comes through with incredible distinction and complicity in this regard: it reactivates a term from Rhenish mysticism, *das Ichts* ("Das Ichts existiert um nichts mehr als das Nichts"), which is *Nichts* minus the N. But the operation is less disruptive from the outset, hence less connected with the signifier; we once again encounter etymology, with the right cut: *n-icht*. However, as no one can be sure which *icht* is involved—demon or essence—we are obliged to hear simultaneously the *Ich,* the "I," which was reformed at the end of the *epoché* and mystical union. Another treasure, another rupture.

To stick with contemporary French, Lacan has Democritus say "*Nothing, perhaps*?—not *perhaps nothing,* but *not nothing.*"[80] I would love to make him say: *Not nothing, but less than nothing*—ot-one, since *hihanappât.*[81]

It must be firmly maintained that this is not a way of founding the one. The *den* can't be tamed inasmuch as it doesn't become a principle. That is why it differs markedly from what Lacan, at almost the same time his attention was focused on it, calls—taking explicit advantage of *nada*—"the nade," or, in capital letters, "the NADE," which comes first before the monad, and is "constituted by the empty set whose breaking through [*franchissement*] is precisely how the One is constituted," "the way in designated by lack," "the place where a hole is made," "the bag with a hole in it" at the "basis of the *Yad'lun*" (*OP* 147).[82] The *den* can only be thought *after* the one, as a subtractive operation, not as an origin, with a hole in it or not. It cannot be dialecticized precisely insofar as it not an assumed and sublated negation of negation but a subtraction after negation and thereby a trick, a fiction, obtained by critical secondarity. It is not a way in but a way *out*, an escape hatch that acts as a stumbling block to philosophy's origin and makes its history, hence that of physics, too, change direction, like the *clinamen* that Lacan compared it to early on.[83]

It is clear that the translations, even the numerous intralinguistic translations, can do nothing but reontologize. Democritus is not a "materialist" (any more, Lacan says, than Freud or you and I are). Moreover, whether in "L'Étourdit," *Encore,* or *The Four Fundamental Concepts,* it is very consistently in connection with idealism that Lacan refers to Freud.

Atomos idea. The atom is an idea. "Atoms, which are also called ideas, are everything" (DK 68 A57, Plutarch, *Against Colotes*, 8, p. 1110F). The idea that is the atom is constantly being distorted into materialism turned back into physics. In this regard I am once again following Heinz Wismann, who takes the expression *atomos idea* as both title and emblem. Aristotle is the true architect of this perverse translation of idealism into materialism, a physics designed to jibe with metaphysics, which is a misinterpretation of Democritus. It is Aristotle who passes atoms off as beings, a little less being than his own being (*étant*), of course (or a little more of a being [*étant*] and a little less being [*être*] on the scale of ontotheology)—in this case, as indivisible, quasi-invisible particles, but the combination of which makes bodies visible. Nevertheless, atoms—stick to your guns, Democritus—are *den*, less than nothing. A vestige of the negation of the one, of identity and of being (*l'étant*), a trajectory of thought; the wave of an ironic operation on being (*l'être*) extending sophistry's operation. Not just one more discourse, more fundamental or fundamentalist, on physics, but a physics of discourse, hence a discourse of another kind on physics, linked to a scathing critique of the ontology that congeals into metaphysics. Atoms are the material name of the elements that make up the logos and are responsible for its power: "The *logos* is a "powerful lord who with the finest and most invisible body[84] [*smikrotatôi sômati kai aphanestatôi*] performs the most divine acts."[85] To say that atomism is a physical representation of discourse is to say that discourse is the proper object of physics or even that the logos is the *phusis* that needs to be described; basically, it is only ever a question of taking seriously the fact that man is an animal endowed with logos, that the nature of man is his culture.

"L'Étourdit" has all the more reason to end with Democritus inasmuch as Democritus, to represent discourse physically, conceived of his atoms as letters. Nothing but ideas, but dreamed up and reconceived each time by the stylus, the hand—if "style is the man," the trace of the stylus is the atom.[86] The properties of the atom refer to the *ductus* of writing, as Heinz Wismann has relentlessly demonstrated, thereby reconnecting with a long, hidden interpretive tradition. Aristotle, who distorted atomism into the physics of elementary bodies, was at once honest and crafty enough not to conceal anything about the model of writing, though he immediately proposed a translation-reduction of it to features that were compatible with those of the bodies in his own physics. That was the start of the great assimilation of atomism. In Book *Alpha* of the *Metaphysics* the three "differences" that are the causes of all the others are so named by Leucippus and Democritus and named again by Aristotle: "These differences [Leucippus and Democritus] say, are three—shape [*skhêma*] and order [*taxin*] and position [*thésin*]. For they say that what is is differentiated only by 'rhythm' [*rhusmôi*] and 'inter-contact' [*diatigêi*] and 'turning' [*tropêi*]; and of these rhythm is shape, inter-contact is order, and turning is position: for *A* differs from *N* in shape, *AN* from *NA* in order, *X* from *E* in position."[87]

"Rhythm"—that of the waves, of the vicissitudes of life, or of people's moods—doesn't connote the "shape" or the "figure," the visible "form" (*skhêma, morphê, eidos*) that enables an object to be self-identical and recognizable to someone looking at it, but the way the object arises out of its own movement, caught up in change and flux the way music is, the ductus of writing that produces one letter rather than another. "Inter-contact" is not the "order" that inscribes succession in space and hierarchy but the points of contact that determine both the way that the ductus divides into sections to form a letter and the way the letters group together to produce words. "Turning," a turn of phrase or a trope, is not the perennial "position" an object occupies in space but the way in which the ductus turns in order to produce the trajectory of a letter, and the inscription of that trajectory in space. Waves and wave propagations, effects and effects of effects, prior to becoming bodies.

Den: the name of the signifier when it is invented as such, being unable to coincide with any signified or referent, is connected with the letter and the presentation of discourse by means of the letter. Such is the scope of the *clam* (secret) that constitutes the complicated workings of "L'Étourdit."

Encore thematizes the first part of the trajectory very clearly: in moving from Aristotle to Democritus, you go from being and the "jouissance of being" (with the whole kit and caboodle, from Saint Thomas to Rousselot, and charity beginning at home) to—if we still have to keep the word *being*—"the being of signifierness" (*l'être de la signifiance*) and its *raison d'être*, "the jouissance of the body":

> What Aristotle wanted to know, and that paved the way for everything that followed in his wake, is what the jouissance of being is . . . Being—if people want me to use this term at all costs—the being that I oppose to that . . . is the being of signifierness. And I fail to see in what sense I am stooping to the ideals of materialism—I say "to the *ideals*" because they're beyond its scope—when I identify the reason for the being of signifierness in jouissance, the jouissance of the body.
>
> But, you see, a body hasn't seemed materialistic enough since Democritus. One has to find atoms and the whole nine yards, not to mention sight, smell, and everything that follows therefrom. All that goes together.
>
> It's no accident that Aristotle occasionally quotes Democritus, even if he feigns disgust when he does so, for he relies on the latter's work. *In fact, the atom is simply an element of flying signifierness, quite simply a* stoikheion.[88]
>
> (*E* 70–71, my emphasis)

The atom is an element of flying signifierness, the way *mana* is a floating signifier: they are signifiers consistent with their being that isn't one, namely, their equivocal being as signifiers, their lack of identity (a *den*ial, if I dare say). For, as we eventually learn, "what distinguishes the signifier is simply the fact that it is what all the others are not;" it shows "the presence of difference as such and nothing else."[89]

The second phase of the trajectory involves inscribing signifierness into the letter, and that is what "L'Étourdit"—which is as incomprehensible as Aristotle is stupid—does. That is why the *den* is necessary, the *den* whose consistency is not an isolated letter like that of Aristotelian propositional logic ("for all x") but a line of letters made up of linked transformations, thus related instead to a small *a* as a phase of a trajectory and connected with any ductus—to the extent that I understand what I'm saying here.

If we somehow manage to think the Real, the real of the principle "there's no such thing as a sexual relationship" in terms (rendered illegible by Aristotle) of the stowaway, the *den,* the stowaway of all ontology, it may actually turn out to be pretty funny.

Ab-sense, the name of the Real as opposed to ontology, is connected with the impasses of logic (the sexual relationship can't be written) and with (the being [*l'être*] of) the letter [*lettre*] as pure wordplay.[90] Of course, the absence of a sexual relationship is responsible for ab-sense being the only course on the menu of the prompter's box. It is no less monotonous, it is even more monotonous, than sense. Except that what its monotonous irruptions—slips, symptoms, and interpretations—have going for them is that they're funny.

As compared with language itself ("The unconscious means nothing if it does not mean that whatever I say, and wherever I'm positioned, even if I'm in a good position,[91] I don't know what I'm saying. . . . Even if I don't know what I'm saying . . . I say that the cause of this is only to be sought in language itself. What I'm adding to Freud . . . I'm adding that the unconscious is structured like a language" [*D* 44]), ab-sense is located right within the relationship between performance and signifier, or: the relationship between performance and signifier defines Lacanian sophistics.

"Now, if there's no such thing as a sexual relationship, we must see in what respect the jouissance of the body can serve a purpose here" (*E* 71).

Postscript
in the form of a few propositions in the future perfect
to respond to what follows

PROPOSITION 1

Linguistricks (*linguisterie*) will not have constituted any more of a Lacanian objection to logology than crookedness (*canaillerie*) has to philosophy—even less, in fact.

Scholium 1

Antiphilosophy, the single name Badiou gives to the whole tradition from Gorgias to Wittgenstein, is characterized, as he himself emphasizes, by the "detection of philosophical crookedness." Crookedness is always a matter of assuming that "there is a metalanguage," an assumption that determines the relationship to Truth.[92] How could Platonic philosophy be an exception to this crooked relationship with Truth when the philosopher-king, even as a fictional construct, deals at least as much with metalanguage as with mathematics?

PROPOSITION 2

The philosophy/antiphilosophy binary will have been a pure product of philosophy, one that philosophy will present as always already having a structuring effect. It is this effect of *always already* (authorizing the always already of being or Being, of truth or Truth, of the real or the Real) that the other discourse, termed "antiphilosophy" by philosophy, reveals.

Scholium 1

Philosophy will always already have won out over antiphilosophy, as soon as it dubs it *anti* (and, in due course, Lacanian analysis, like Kantian critique or Hegelian dialectics, will only reinforce the binary). What I call logology rather than antiphilosophy abhors the binarism that always makes the other term fall on the other side, thereby ensuring the prominence of the first term (which will then be referred to as the philosopheme "pure being as unbound multiplicity")[93] on the model of sense (everything that is outside-sense [*hors-sens*] is either meaningful or senseless [*sensé ou inane*]), which is precisely what we must take our distance from. Logology makes use of (il)logical relativism, which is linked to both the dedicated, i.e., strategic, comparative of "better for" and the best way to inscribe plurality, including inscribing it politically.

Scholium 2

Clearly, the requirement that logology and philosophy have in common stipulates "absence of sense," with the difference between ab-sense and non-sense being maintained. Isn't this difference demonstrated otherwise (and much better) by Democritus's *den* than by the formula? If the function of the formula is to make it understood that ab-sense is ab-sex sense (linked to the impossibility of writing the sexual relationship), then the *den* will be the formula's stowaway, preventing one kind of monotony (no contradiction) from being replaced by another (no sexual relationship). Indeed, it will then be said that "a topology is deployed where it is the word that decides the matter" (8; 452).[94]

PROPOSITION 3

It will have been convenient, but no more than that, for philosophy to handle the man/woman difference by tacking it onto the philosophy/antiphilosophy difference.

Scholium 1

In particular, one won't (or won't only) conclude that antiphilosophy/the woman-philosopher does no more than "present philosophy with a new object" (plasticity, sophistics, etc.), brought back to the center from the margins, which is tantamount to reinforcing the center's centrality and creating a beautiful history of twentieth- or twenty-first-century philosophy.[95] Because it is not an object that is at issue but how an object is dealt with, and, more precisely, how the permeability of genres, including those of philosophy and antiphilosophy, is dealt with. And this has consequences for knowledge as well as for the mastery it confers.

Scholium 2

Since we're in good company here (we've all read Lacan), it will be understood that a woman can be a man-philosopher and that a man can be a woman-philosopher. It remains to be seen whether philosophers and antiphilosophers, or philosophers and logologists, will understand in the same way that for a woman "the word 'truth' provokes a certain shiver" and "she will benefit much more than the man does from . . . a [certain] culture of discourse" (*OS* 55 [translation modified]).

PRINCIPLE:

There's No Such Thing as a Sexual Relationship
"L'Étourdit"

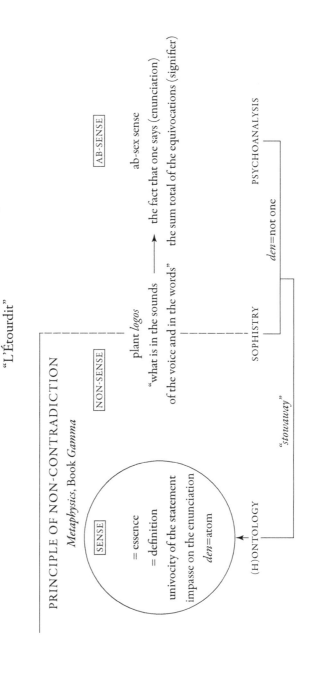

Formulas of "L'Étourdit"

ALAIN BADIOU

The word *formulas* in my title "For-
mulas of 'L'Étourdit'" should no doubt be understood in two different
senses. First, to be sure, in the sense of mathematical formulas, which
lies behind the phrase "formulas of sexuation." Second, in Rimbaud's
poetic sense: "I have found the place and the formula."[1] We need to think
about the relationship between these two senses. How can a formula be
at one and the same time in the register of the matheme and in that of
a subject's existence?

It has often been said—and in this book, Barbara Cassin says
it again to perfection—that psychoanalysis in general and Lacan in
particular play on the ambiguities of the signifier. It has been said that
Lacan's understanding of language is completely deontologized because

the ambiguity of the signifier and the plurality of interpretations destroy one of the basic concepts of philosophical ontology from Aristotle to Deleuze—with Badiou only making matters worse—namely, the univocity of being.

But "formulas" raises an objection to this point of view, because a formula, on the contrary, is a proposition of univocity so absolute that its literal universality is blatantly obvious. From which it follows that if the other of psychoanalysis and Lacan is assumed to be Aristotle's metaphysics, it must immediately be conceded that it's not because that metaphysics supports the univocity of being but because Aristotle didn't understand (and, to that extent, Plato was better) that the safeguarding of univocity can only be entrusted to mathematical literality, the paradigm of every hole punched by truth in the inadequacy of meaning (*sens*)[2]—and the discursive real of the ontology of the multiple, to boot.

It is only through the test of formalization—I'll come back to this later—that sense, touched by the real, brings about truth as ab-sense.

And the real will be called being, bare being. To that extent, even though he called it "hontology," Lacan could no more do without an ontology than anyone else could. An ontology even safer from being reduced to the logology that my very dear friend Barbara suggested be substituted for ontological reverie (or "bullshit" [*connerie*]?) which Lacan was undoubtedly the first to condemn in the "linguistic turn" dropped into America by the Viennese and which he so splendidly termed "idea-linguistricks" (*idéalinguisterie*).

Would we only have a choice between the vacuity of ontology and the idealism of logology?

This is not the dilemma in which Lacan is caught, since, far from the ambiguity of meaning being the unsurpassable horizon of his thinking, it is "formalization," he says, "that is our goal, our ideal."[3]

As far as Lacan is concerned, even though the course of an analysis is the realm of ambiguity, its ultimate goal, as we know, is a knowledge that is integrally transmissible, transmissible without remainder. The goal is an order of symbolization or, as he puts it, of "correct formalization," in which there is no longer any trace of ambiguity.

I would like to focus my remarks on a difficult question: how is the transition from linguistic ambiguity to something—the formula or formalization—that is both its boundary and its negation effected in psychoanalysis? What is the hole in ambiguous language that brings the void of univocity to the surface? I want to focus on this question—the hole that formalized univocity drills in hermeneutic ambiguity—because I think "L'Étourdit" is fundamentally focused on it as well.

A good deal of "L'Étourdit" is devoted to the question of the matheme, the question of mathematical relations. Lacan no doubt hits on the key issue when he wonders how to get from (imaginary) impotence to (real) impossibility in the analytic treatment.[4] However, that relationship is unintelligible, as the text explains, if we don't examine what a formalization is.

My only direct citation from "L'Étourdit," a passage on which everything I'm going to say will be a commentary, can be found on either page 8 or page 452, depending on which edition (the text originally published in *Scilicet* or the one reprinted in *Autres écrits*) you are using. Here it is:

> Freud tips us off to the fact that ab-sense denotes sex: it's when this ab-sex sense is most inflated that a topology is deployed in which it's the word that decides.[5]
> [Freud nous met sur la voie de ce que l'ab-sens désigne le sexe: c'est à la gonfle de ce sens-absexe qu'une topologie se déploie où c'est le mot qui tranche.]

I'll let this glow in the darkness of its literal meaning for the time being and just tell you what my main theme is going to be. As usual, it will be an investigation of Lacan's relationship with philosophy.

Ultimately, that's the only thing that interests me. And it's only natural. I've pointed out in a variety of texts, and especially in my recent

Wittgenstein's Antiphilosophy,[6] that those who claim to be antiphilosophers, as do Wittgenstein, Lacan, and, basically, under the name of "sophistics," Barbara Cassin, are merely issuing to philosophy the special challenge of a new object that they say single-handedly dethrones philosophy's established pretensions, since philosophy has "forgotten about" or dispensed with investigating this object. To that end, these antiphilosophers *present* the extraordinary object in question to philosophy, whether it is nonbeing (Gorgias), the wager (Pascal), pure existence (Rousseau), the radical choice (Kierkegaard), life (Nietzsche), language (Wittgenstein), or the unconscious (Lacan). And this presentation of the object quickly inscribes the antiphilosophers in a special variation of philosophy.

I have, I believe, contributed to this inevitable reinscription of Lacan into philosophy as such. And the point where he is reinscribed is none other than the critique of meaning, or sense, in favor of a knowledge of the real. Doing away with sense is without a doubt the loftiest concern of any philosophy worthy of the name. Indeed, truth, the love of which, as we know, is the basis of all philosophy, is incompatible with the variability of sense, with its unreliability. Yes, we seek the ab-sence of sense.

Yet in every antiphilosopher there remains a remnant, which means that, from within his/her reinscription into philosophy, the uniqueness of his/her dissent still glimmers here and there, a reminder that s/he was once an "anti." In Lacan's case, it involves not regarding or wanting "truth" to be that whereby all knowledge maintains that it touches some real.

So my investigation will be an investigation of Lacan the philosopher as an antiphilosopher. Or as a philosopher owing to the fact that psychoanalysis is antiphilosophical, as are the sciences in general, but without for all that providing any reason, any more than do the sciences, to conclude that antiphilosophy has triumphed. Quite the contrary: trying too hard to ensure that knowledge alone triumphs paves new ways for truth to triumph.

My investigation will therefore be carried out on the basis of the following conceptual triad: truth, knowledge, real. I maintain that

"L'Étourdit" is a disjunction between the discourse of analysis and the discourse of philosophy with respect to two entirely different ways of putting together the truth/knowledge/real triad, a triad that is in fact—provided its terms are not rearranged—common to both discourses, the philosopher's and the analyst's. Indeed, this triad is the dividing line between the two discourses.

What is the true nature of the philosophical operation, in Lacan's view? What does Lacan identify as "philosophical" so that his antiphilosophy can assume its full meaning? The philosophical operation, for Lacan, consists in asserting that there is a meaning of truth. But why does philosophy claim there is a meaning of truth? Because its objective, the consolation it offers us under the name of "wisdom," is to be able to say that there is a truth of the real. That is its implicit or explicit axiom: there is a meaning of truth because there is a truth of the real. So, against what he considers to be the very operation of philosophy, Lacan will argue, in "L'Étourdit" in particular and contrary to what he occasionally argued before, that *there is no meaning of truth because there is no truth of the real*. "L'Étourdit's" argument is that, when it comes to the real, there is only a knowledge function. There is a knowledge function and it is not of the order of truth as such.

The real, in "L'Étourdit," is clearly definable on the basis of the absence of sense. As a result, in order for the truth/knowledge/real triad to be thought through thoroughly it has to be shifted around in relation to the question of sense. In her brilliant commentary on Book *Gamma* of Aristotle's *Metaphysics*, Barbara Cassin speaks of a "decision of meaning." Indeed, it could be said that "L'Étourdit" is another decision of meaning, distinct from the Aristotelian one. With regard to this decision, the real may be defined as *sense* qua *ab-sense*. The real is ab-sense, hence absence of sense, which obviously implies that there is such a thing as sense.

The point that needs to be understood concerning the complex decision Lacan is making here is that ab-sense must be absolutely distinguished from non-sense. Lacan's is not an absurdist argument or an

existential one in the broad sense of the term. It is not an assertion of
the non-sense of the real. Rather, it is an assertion that an access to the
real can be opened only if it is assumed that the real is like an absence in
sense, an ab-sense, or a subtraction of, or from, sense. Everything hinges
on the distinction between ab-sense and non-sense.

Why is this issue of prime concern to psychoanalysis in its quarrel
with philosophy? Quite simply because you can only grasp the distinction
between absence and non-sense through its correlation with sex, or, more
precisely, through its correlation with what constitutes the entire real of
the unconscious, namely, the fact that there's no such thing as a sexual
relationship. Sex proposes—nakedly, if I may put it this way—the real as
the impossible proper: the impossibility of a relationship. The impossible,
hence the real, is thus linked to ab-sense and, in particular, to the absence
of any relationship, which means the absence of any sexual meaning. There
is a logical genealogy: the real can be expressed as impossibility proper
in terms of sense qua ab-sense, and that is why one of the synonyms for
ab-sense in Lacan's text is "ab-sex sense." "Ab-sex sense" is a formula, the
formula expressing that there's no such thing as a sexual relationship. And
it is of the utmost importance to understand that the negative expressions
("there's no such thing as," "there's such a thing as ab-sense") are equivalent
to a non-negative formula, namely, "ab-sex sense."

Absence as subtraction from sense or from the classical decision
of sense (for example, the sexual "relationship" is devoid of sense and is
therefore not a relationship) cannot be classified with sense or with the
Aristotelian-type decision of sense. But nor can it be classified, via a negative reversal, with non-sense. Actually, it is neither sense nor non-sense
but a unique, incongruous, and absolutely original proposition, namely,
ab-sense, absence of sense. But absence of sense, in *positive* terms, means
ab-sex sense, that is, in the final analysis, the real as having this absence
of sense whereby there's no such thing as a relationship, a sexual relationship in this case, which the syntactic formula of ab-sex sense encapsulates

affirmatively. This is the key proposition of "L'Étourdit": the absence of sense isn't non-sense because it is ab-sex sense.

The critical significance of this proposition is that it founds the possibility of the matheme, of integral transmission—in short, of the formula. It founds that possibility by positing that *any function of the real in knowledge concerns, in positive terms, absence.* When all is said and done, what is integrally transmissible is always an inscription of absence as ab-sex sense. This is essentially the general form of the formulas of knowledge: a knowledge function on the real is a function that concerns ab-sense inasmuch as it is based positively on ab-sex sense. It could then be said that there is indeed a meaning of knowledge. Knowledge qua knowledge as a function in the real is endowed with this unique sense—ab-sex sense or ab-sense. Consequently, the relation to the real that Lacan proposes as that of the discourse of the analyst will be a relation of a meaning of knowledge qua ab-sex sense, whereas the philosophical relation to the real is in the register of truth.

At this stage, Lacan's assessment of philosophy is that it is incapable of attaining the meaning of knowledge. Led astray by that fatal symptom, the love of truth, philosophy fails to grasp the principle by which something of meaning is linked to knowledge in the function of the real, in what makes a formula out of "there's no such thing as a sexual relationship." Philosophy fails to grasp that absolutely unique sense that is, strictly speaking, neither sense nor non-sense but ab-sex sense. This obviously means that philosophy fails to grasp the real, even in terms of the givenness of the real that consists in gaining access to a meaning of knowledge. Philosophy could also be said to be precipitated, as it were, out of truth. And this precipitation conceals or eliminates the time of the real as absence, hence as a "knowing" relationship with ab-sex sense.[7]

To put it another, or simpler, way: philosophy is trapped in the sense-truth pair, which assumes that the opposite of sense is non-sense, not ab-sense. This is why philosophy is a search for the meaning of truth, for the sole purpose of avoiding the existential drama of non-sense.

We should note in passing that this unusual accusation against philosophy differs from the one Lacan leveled against religion. Religion isn't the endless search for a meaning of truth because religion is the proposition that, in one respect at least, truth and meaning are indistinguishable from each other. There is no meaning of truth as a defense against non-sense; instead, there is a Supreme Being whose formula is truth = meaning. Unlike religion, philosophy is not required to maintain that, in one respect at least, meaning and truth are indistinguishable from each other. It *may* do so, of course, but that is not its essence. Philosophy is locked in a sort of face-off between meaning and truth. There is not necessarily any interpretation of truth as meaning in philosophy, nor is there necessarily any religiosity. It is impossible to displace the meaning-truth pair, because the only thing that can budge it is the category of ab-sense or ab-sex sense as a function of the real. In philosophy there is thus no function of the real in knowledge on account of this absolute primordiality of a confrontation between truth and sense, such that the essential "there's no such thing," in which the impossibility of the real is attested, is ultimately sidestepped.

So if we don the robes of philosophy's attorney—robes that, to speak in the manner of Joseph Prudhomme,[8] fit me like a glove—we can begin the defense this way: Lacan's whole antiphilosophical critique is based on the validity, the relevance, or the force of the category of ab-sense or of ab-sex sense. More precisely, everything hinges on the claim that psychoanalysis, through its experience of sex, of ab-sex, encounters a real that displaces the effects of sense to such an extent that it can affirm that there is a register of sense that is neither the affirmation of sense nor its negation. Analytic experience is assumed to open up a space between sense and non-sense, a space that is required for the analytic act to be able to crystallize.

The very existence of the analytic act, we should remember, can only be verified after the fact.[9] After what fact? The production of a transmissible knowledge. Only such a production can prove retroactively that something like an analytic act occurred.[10] There may have been something like one without it, but it won't have been proven. Yet such a transmissible knowledge is clearly a function of knowledge in the real. So it concerns ab-sex sense or ab-sense in one way or another. Regardless of whether we consider things from the standpoint of theory, of antiphilosophy, or from the standpoint of the clinic, we always come back to the absolute necessity, in Lacan's teaching, for a gap to be able to open up between sense and non-sense. This is in fact where the real as such is ultimately located, the real of the "there's no such thing," the real as the impossibility of a relationship, or—let me venture the philosopheme—pure being as unbound multiplicity. Or the void.

Moreover, it was in regard to this issue that debates raged in the psychoanalytic schools about one of Lacan's great inventions, the pass. This procedure is used to verify that something like an analytic act occurred. It is based entirely on the idea of transmissibility, of transmissible knowledge. Through the test of successive transmissions, the procedure verifies that something like knowledge, hence a function of the real, was produced during an analytic treatment. The standard practice involves someone telling someone else what happened and this other person telling it to a third person. In this way an effective transmissibility filters through, a transmissibility from which any dubious remnants have been eliminated owing to the fact that it occurs in several stages. What interests me about all this is that the opening of a space between sense and non-sense, such that ab-sex sense can emerge in a position of minimum accessibility, is confirmed, after the fact, by a transmissibility related to the analytic act. The act can never be presented in a proposition. It coincides with its own taking-place.[11] The aspect of the act that can be indirectly inscribed in the form of a transmissible knowledge has to constitute proof of the act itself. The act can only be attested in the form of the transmissibility of knowledge. Why? Because such knowledge concerns absence or ab-sex sense. So you could say that the pass is the transitive organization, lodged in speech, of successive absences. It is a device holding together—or not (if they don't "pass")—accounts whose immanent organization is presumed to be located in ab-sex sense so as to verify that the transmission is really the transmission of a knowledge functioning in the real.

Ultimately, Lacan is convinced that *philosophy, in exemplary fashion, is that which doesn't "pass," that of which there can be no pass.* That's precisely why there are only masters and disciples in philosophy. No philosopher is going to tell someone his/her philosophy on condition that that person tell it to someone else and that this other person certify before a committee that the original speaker is indeed a philosopher, that a philosophical act somehow occurred. The accusation leveled against philosophy is that if you are in a face-off between meaning and truth—as philosophy claims to be, unaware as it is of the "there's no such thing as a relationship"— you are not able to produce knowledge that is transmissible integrally and without remainder. You can't come up with the formula, since any formula requires a knowledge that is a function of the real. Indeed, as far as the psychoanalyst is concerned, philosophy doesn't pass. This can in fact be expressed the other way around: the waste products of a pass are no doubt composed of philosophemes. If we rummage through the trash of the pass, we'll find some philosophical waste material in a fairly advanced state of decomposition. The hard kernel of the pass is that which testifies to a real in the guise of ab-sex sense that has been touched by an act. The waste products are generally untransmissible philosophemes strewn around the edges of sense or non-sense.

Lacan's antiphilosophy can ultimately be expressed in three different ways.

First, philosophy lacks any awareness of the register of ab-sense. It doesn't want to know anything about that register. Philosophy invariably substitutes something else for ab-sense or ab-sex sense. Thus, as Barbara

Cassin has shown, Aristotle brings in the principle of noncontradiction in its place.

Second, philosophy knows nothing about the function of knowledge in the real. It absorbs it in the love of truth.

And third, there is a specular quality to philosophy because it arranges meaning and truth as mirror images under the guise of saying that there may possibly be a meaning of truth.

We can return, then, to the knowledge-truth-real triad as it functions in the formulas of "L'Étourdit."

For Lacan, there is no truth of the real, contrary to what is always assumed one way or another by philosophy. There is truth only insofar as there is a function of the real in knowledge.

Furthermore, there is, strictly speaking, no knowledge of the real either. There is a function of the real in knowledge, but that's not at all the same thing. Knowledge is, of course, produced in the element of ab-sex sense, but it isn't knowledge of ab-sex sense as such.

Finally, there is no knowledge of truth either. At most it might be said that there is truth of knowledge to the extent that a real is functioning within it. Let's say—this is a convention like any other—that the truth of knowledge can be gauged by the fact that something of the real of ab-sex sense is functioning in it. But this doesn't mean there is any knowledge of truth.

Consequently, for Lacan—and this, I think, is the most original, important thesis in "L'Étourdit"—the knowledge-truth-real triad cannot be broken up. It can't be split up into pairs. It can't be arranged into pairs such as truth of the real, knowledge of the real, or knowledge of truth. According to Lacan, every time you talk about truth in psychoanalysis it is really knowledge and the real that ought to be brought up. Every time you talk about knowledge it is truth and the real that should be brought up. And it is impossible to talk about the real without bringing up truth and knowledge. The truth-knowledge-real triad is an indivisible one. If you claim that there are such things as truth and the real, you have to situate the knowledge function in relation to them; if you have knowledge of the real, you must assume that there is a truth effect; and when you talk about the relations between truth and knowledge, the real has to be taken into account.

Things become much clearer then. Ultimately, for Lacan, the philosophical operation amounts to breaking up the triad, contending that the triad can be arranged into pairs. Why? Well, because in assuming that there can be a truth of the real, philosophy also assumes there can be a knowledge of truth and that, for this very reason, it can put the three pairs of the triad back together again after breaking it up. I could show how, whenever these issues are discussed in "L'Étourdit"—but also in the network of texts surrounding it that Lacan wrote between 1970 and 1975—it is always a matter for him of putting the triad back together. It needs to be recovered at the vanishing point of its arrangement into philosophical pairs. The indissolubility of the truth-knowledge-real triad has to be restored and any possibility of a face-off between only two of its terms avoided.

I will thus propose the following Lacanian definition of philosophy to you. Philosophy is a subversion of the three by the two. Philosophy refuses to accept that the three is irreducibly originary, that it is impossible to reduce it to the two. This, in my opinion, is the reason for the continuous, complex dispute between Lacan and Hegel, since Hegel proposed a position of the three that is necessarily engendered by the two. But which two? The two of contradiction. It is in this sense that Hegel was the most philosophical of philosophers for Lacan.

Except, what should be added, what constitutes the ultimate mystery whose meaning we need to elucidate, is that *the quarrel over the three and the two, when all is said and done, is a quarrel over the One.* Let me propose a Lacanian theorem here, which, though not exactly Lacan's, can still serve as an essential antiphilosophical theorem. This theorem can be formulated as follows: "If you subvert the three by the two it's because you have a wrong idea of the One." And how is this wrong idea in turn formulated? Well, it's formulated as "The One is!" As soon as you say "The One is," you're on your way to subverting the three by the two. Hegel already had to assert the being of the Absolute as the One-position of the becoming of Spirit in order to set in motion the negative, which in turn engenders the three from simple contradiction. If you claim "The One is," you're on your way to breaking up the originary truth-knowledge-real triad, because, in the final analysis, to say "The One is" comes down to saying that there is a truth of the real insofar as the real is One. Where the real manifests the unity of its being is where the real truth of the real can be found. That is the first pair extracted from the three. Likewise, to say "The One is" is also to claim that there is a knowledge of the real: the knowledge of the One in the guise of the object or of objectivity. That's the second pair extracted from the three. Thus as soon as you say "the One is" you are in the sphere of philosophy.

If, on the other hand, the real is not something of which there can be truth, nor is it something that can be known, i.e., if none of those philosophical pairs—truth of the real, knowledge of the real, and truth of that knowledge—are extracted from the triad, then the statement about the One cannot be "The One is." Instead, it will be the statement "There is something of (the) One" (*Il y a de l'Un*). The "there is something of (the) One" is a radical subversion of the speculative, or philosophical, thesis "The One is."

A great many of Lacan's arguments are intended to show that if you claim that there is something of (the) One rather than that the One is, then you are not involved in breaking up the triad. The cohesion of the three can be maintained in the form of truth-knowledge-real. It's just that you need to understand what, in a way, is going to guarantee the triad's indivisible connectedness. And since it can't be one of the components of the triad—truth or knowledge—because we would then be reverting to the philosophical pairs, the inevitable consequence is that the triad's cohesion will hinge on the interplay between the real, the "exceptional" point, or "out-of-place" (*hors-lieu*),[12] of the triad, and something that, being neither truth nor knowledge, is necessarily in the dimension of the act.

Since there is neither knowledge (*connaissance*)[13] nor truth of the real, and since, on the contrary, there is truth provided only that it is inextricably linked to the real in the guise of a knowledge (*savoir*) function, there has to be a pure encounter with this real. Let's call the point where the real as such is encountered an "act."

The real is impossible to know (*connaître*) precisely because it is embedded in the truth-knowledge-real triad and can't be extracted from it in order to be paired with one of the other two terms. You even always have to say about the real that it "supplants knowing" (*dépose le connaître*). Lacan calls this supplanting of knowing the "demonstration" of the real, which is a pretty strange word, albeit a very compelling one. The real cannot be known; it must be demonstrated.

But how, then, does Lacan avoid Kantianism? Because, if the real is inaccessible to knowing (*le connaître*), we enter the realm of critical exegesis, which declares the real (the in-itself) to be unknowable (*inconnaissable*) and reserves knowledge (*le savoir*) exclusively for phenomena. Ultimately, reality would be the phenomenal givenness of things, and the real would be its point of inaccessibility, to which one would simply relate through the act, i.e., to which one would have a practical relationship. There would be a prescriptive relationship to the real, not at all a cognitive one. The real is given in practical reason, in the categorical imperative, not in theoretical reason, which orders phenomena. There are readings of Lacan and Kant—the Slovenian readings (Žižek, Zupančič, Riha, Šumič et al.)—that take this approach and are very persuasive.

I, for one, think Lacan dodges the trap of criticism and is in no way a Kantian. The feat he accomplishes is to propose neither that the real is unknowable nor that it is knowable. Lacan's thesis is that the real is external to the antimony of knowing and not-knowing. The real, as such, does not stem from the binary categories of knowing and not-knowing. Rather, it is related to what Lacan attempts to invent with the word *demonstrating*.

"Demonstrating the real" can be understood in two different senses.[14] To some extent, of course, it is the doctrine—which is altogether classical in Lacan—that there is no science of the real except a logical, a formal, science. The real will be defined as an impasse of formalization. What touches the real, then, is lucid, perfectly pure formalization. As a result, the only possible transmissibility of ab-sex sense is found in the form of the matheme. There is no language of the real; there are only formulas. The second sense of "demonstrating the real," as I've said, is that access to the real opens up in the dimension of the act. The paramount issue, then, is the "relations"—with all the scare quotes you like—between act and matheme. This is where the fate of if not Lacan's whole theory then at least its confrontation with philosophy is decided: in the ability to grasp as a singular way of thinking a type of space shared by the matheme and the analytic act. And I've shown that the pass is one aspect of this question.

Let's say that "something like psychoanalysis" occurred, or even that there was a psychoanalyst, if someone was there where the act authorizes the matheme.

It remains for us to ask whether there is any guarantee as to an outcome "in" truth of the process constituted by the indivisibility of the triad and the access to the real by means of the formulas and in accordance with the act. A guarantee that would be like a sign, a signal, that we are indeed in the element of ab-sex sense, or of ab-sense, and that the real can therefore answer in its place.[15]

Well, the answer is yes, there is. According to Lacan, there has long been a sign of all this, and that sign is anxiety. This affect acts as an implicit guarantee of the truth effect produced by the function of knowledge in the real. Like Pascal, Rousseau, and Kierkegaard, Lacan maintains that there is no disjunction between the primacy of the act and the potential transparency of saying (*du dire*). This is not just a trivial matter of some miraculous irrationality of the act standing in opposition to any rational transmissibility of saying. Rather, it is the idea that there is a point, no doubt an enigmatic one, but, in any case, always unique and always having to be reclaimed, never given in advance—for example, the experience of the analytic treatment for Lacan or the experience of the wager and conversion for Pascal or the experience of the various aesthetic, ethical, and religious stages for Kierkegaard—there is a point, then, at which the cut induced by the act and the integral transmissibility of saying are linked together in a sort of mysterious pairing, which is, at the same time, no more than a moment in the becoming of thought. And this point is signaled by an affect, an affect that cannot deceive us. As Lacan said, very early on, "Anxiety is that which does not deceive."[16]

For Lacan, this has consequences concerning what might be called the ethics of the analytic treatment. In the course of an analysis there are two requirements that are in tension with each other. The first of these is to induce, or produce, what Lacan calls a "correct formalization." A correct formalization can be defined as the raising of (imaginary) impotence to (real) impossibility. You have to produce a field of capture, meaning a field of encounter, of the real. But for that to happen, for the real to be able to come (back) to a point, you need to have a formalized system of constraints designating the point of impossibility to be arrived at in one way or another.

And then, says Lacan, there is another requirement, one that has to do with anxiety. I already mentioned Lacan's very compelling dictum about this: "Anxiety is that which does not deceive." The problem is that this affect—which is essentially the affect of the real-knowledge-truth triad subject to the law of the real—must be used in moderation. The right amount of anxiety has to be meted out. It is the analyst's responsibility to moderate the dosage (which is lethal in excess) of what doesn't deceive, of what indicates that we're getting close to ab-sex sense, close to what opens up between sense and non-sense as a new possibility.

So there are two intertwined temporalities in the analytic treatment. First, that of formalization, which is always tempted to be precipitous, always tempted by haste, by the lure of speedy formalization. And then, in the second place, you have the time of the proper dosing of anxiety. This kind of time, on the contrary, is always tempted by the interminable. That is in fact one of the meanings of Freud's well-known title, *Analysis Terminable and Interminable*. The temporality that involves meting out anxiety is one that may keep on deferring the real and linger on the border between sense and non-sense, which are ultimately one and the same in that they both have to avoid the ab-sense of sex. On the other hand, when it comes to formalization, the psychoanalyst's temptation is to avoid his or her own destitution. S/he enjoys quickly achieving the brilliance of a hasty formalization. These two temporalities are interwoven, intertwined. The ethics of the analytic treatment probably consists in holding on to these conflicting temporal injunctions, holding on to them until such time as the act settles the matter. Only the act, which consigns the triad to its own formula, can cut through the intertwined times of the analytic treatment—the act of which, as we know, the psychoanalyst will be no more than the waste product.

So now I can conclude with what is surely the truest distinction between psychoanalysis and philosophy, a distinction for which "L'Étourdit" provides the formulas. In the analytic treatment, owing to its indivisible relationship with the truth-knowledge-real triad, there is an immanent relation between haste and restraint.[17] This relation entails a dialectical link between the formulas as products of the desire for the matheme (correct formalization) and the affect (anxiety) as the guarantee of the real. Thus, in their temporal dialectic, matheme and anxiety are the contrasting figures of the deferred access to the real, an access that, as a braid woven out of a time always suspended between haste and stagnation, will in the end be decided, in the guise of the act, by the analysand him- or herself.

Philosophy couldn't care less about this external decision,[18] in which the act constitutes the silent incision of an unknown truth,[19] since philosophy's distinctive temporal hallmark is that it has *all the time in the world*. This has always served to identify in its discourse the antidialectical connection it has with the eternity of Truth.

Psychoanalysis is not at all concerned with that connection, whose inaugural proposition, which Lacan shares, is that truth has no meaning, but whose further development posits that, as regards *a* truth, insofar as it belongs to the register of *Truth*, and without there being the slightest knowledge of the latter, there is nothing to prevent us from saying everything we can about it, since it is in no way constituted by the act of saying. Philosophy, on the other hand, can operate freely without abandoning any of its speculative ambition *with respect to psychoanalysis* and without having to jettison (along with ontology, for the sake of the dubious properties of language) its conviction that a truth, however outside-sense (*hors-sens*) or ab-sense it may be, is nonetheless a pure contact with the real.

Thus, and on this basis, Lacan unwillingly becomes, like Gorgias, Pascal, Rousseau, Kierkegaard, Nietzsche, and Wittgenstein before him, and like Barbara Cassin after him, a subtle metaphysician.

Notes

INTRODUCTION TO *THERE'S NO SUCH THING AS*
A SEXUAL RELATIONSHIP

1. Charles Melman, "What Thrilled Me in Fierens' Book," *The
   Letter* 41 (2009): 121.
2. Cormac Gallagher's translation was published in *The
   Letter* 41, 43, 45, 49 and 50; it is available at http://www.
   lacaninireland.com/web/published-works/ecrits. A translation by Jack Stone ("et al.") is available here: http://web.
   missouri.edu/~stonej/L%27Etourdit.pdf. Anthony Chadwick's translation is available here: http://www.scribd.com/
   doc/56094420/Etourdit-Integrated.

3. Papers from the conference that Gallagher organized on
"L'Étourdit" in May 2009 were published in *The Letter: The
Irish Journal for Lacanian Psychoanalysis* and are available
here: http://whatispsychoanalysis.ie/category/archive-2/
page/2/.

4. In this form, it resembles the third person singular of the
verb *étourdir*, meaning "to daze" or "to stun," as in *il étourdit*
("he stuns"); preceded by *l'* it could mean "(he or she) dazes
or stuns it [or *him* or *her*]." But it lacks a pronoun or noun
needed to indicate the subject of the utterance. Lacan's
addition of a final *t* also makes the last syllable spell *dit*,
the third-person singular of the verb *dire*, that is, "says," as
well as its past participle, "said." The distinction between
le dire (the saying, that is, the act of saying) and *le dit* (the
said) is central to "L'Étourdit."

5. In *L'oeuvre claire: Lacan, la science, la philosophie* (Paris: Seuil,
1995) Jean-Claude Milner distinguishes between Lacan's
"first classicism" (which finds its *summa* in the publication
of *Écrits* in 1966) and the "second classicism" (beginning in
the 1970s and achieving its definitive statement in Seminar
XX: *Encore*, in 1972–73). The first classicism is based on
structural linguistics, and emphasizes the relationship of the
orders of the symbolic and the imaginary, and the second
shifts to mathematical concepts drawn primarily from set
theory and topology, and subordinates the imaginary and
the symbolic to the real. In her essay "Desuturing Desire:
The Work of the Letter in the Miller-Leclaire Debate,"
Tracy McNulty criticizes this division of Lacan's thinking,
pointing out that the Lacanian clinic always involved all
three orders (real, symbolic, imaginary), and that even such
notoriously "late" concepts as the Borromean knot appear
already in Lacan's work in the 1950s. In *Concept and Form,*

vol. 2: *Interviews and Essays on "Cahiers pour l'Analyse,"* ed.
Peter Hallward and Knox Peden (London: Verso, 2012).

6. The published texts by Lacan most helpful for reading
"L'Étourdit" are *The Seminar of Jacques Lacan. Book XX,
Encore: On Feminine Sexuality, The Limits of Love and
Knowledge, 1972–1973,* ed. Jacques-Alain Miller and trans.
Bruce Fink (New York: Norton, 1998) and *Le Séminaire,
livre XIX . . . ou pire,* text established by Jacques-Alain Miller
(Paris: Seuil, 2011). Cormac Gallagher's unofficial transla-
tion of Seminar XIX (and most of Lacan's other seminars)
is available on his Web site: http://www.lacaninireland.
com/web/.

7. Badiou presents a brief account of his writings on Lacan in
the introduction to his seminar, *Lacan: L'antiphilosophie
3, 1994–1995* (7–10), which was published by Fayard in
2013; the English translation is forthcoming with Columbia
University Press. In "Philosophy as Biography," published
in the online journal *The Symptom*, Badiou talks about his
"three masters," Sartre, Lacan, and Althusser. About Lacan
he writes, "Lacan taught me the connection, the necessary
link between a theory of subjects and a theory of forms.
He taught me how and why the very thinking of subjects,
which had so often been opposed to the theory of forms,
was in reality intelligible only within the framework of this
theory. He taught me that the subject is a question that is not
at all of a psychological character, but is an axiomatic and
formal question. More than any other question!" (http://
www.lacan.com/symptom9_articles/badiou19.html).

8. Translations of the two essays, "Mark and Lack" (1968) and
"Infinitesimal Subversion" (1969), are included in *Concept
and Form:* vol. 1, *Selections from the "Cahiers pour l'Analyse,"*
ed. Peter Hallward and Knox Peden (London: Verso, 2012).

Badiou's *Le concept de modèle* (Paris: Maspéro, 1969) was published in English as *The Concept of Model: An Introduction to the Materialist Epistemology of Mathematics,* ed. and trans. Zachary Luke Fraser and Tzuchien Tho (Melbourne: Re.press, 2007). Badiou and Élisabeth Roudinesco have published a small book of dialogues, *Jacques Lacan: Past and Present,* trans. Jason E. Smith (New York: Columbia University Press, 2014), and Badiou has written numerous other essays on psychoanalysis and Lacan, including three chapters on "Philosophy and Psychoanalysis" in *Conditions,* trans. Steven Corcoran (New York: Continuum, 2008).

9. *L'Effet sophistique* (Paris: Gallimard, 1995).

10. Barbara Cassin, *Jacques le sophiste: Lacan, logos et psych- analyse* (Paris: EPEL, 2012). A volume of essays in English drawn from various aspects of Cassin's work has appeared recently; see *Sophistical Practice: Toward a Consistent Relativism* (New York: Fordham University Press, 2014). Also see her *Voir Hélène en toute femme: D'Homère à Lacan* (Paris: Les Empêcheurs de penser en rond, 2000). Finally, we must mention Barbara Cassin's monumental editorial project, *Dictionary of Untranslatables: A Philosophical Lexicon* (Princeton: Princeton University Press, 2014), which includes numerous invaluable accounts of Lacanian ideas and terms.

11. In his seminar . . . *ou pire*, Lacan remarks that "the absence of the sexual relationship obviously doesn't interfere with a liaison, far from it, but gives it its conditions" (*OP* 19).

12. In his Seminar XX: *Encore* (78), Lacan draws a diagram on the board to illustrate the lack of a sexual relationship and the modes of jouissance available to men and women. On the man's side (the left) we find the matheme for the subject, $, which addresses the *objet a* on the side of the woman. On

the woman's side (the right), the $\overline{La}$ (the feminine article in French, translated as "woman" with a bar through it to indicate that Woman as such, as a totality, does not exist) addresses the matheme for the phallus, Φ, on the man's side. A woman's "supplementary jouissance" is indicated by the other arrow that points from her to the matheme $S(\cancel{A})$, the signifier of the lack in the Other, that is, the symbolic order's inconsistency. Lacan will refer to this as "the jouissance of the Other," "the Other jouissance," and "feminine jouissance" in *Encore*.

13. Lacan develops the idea of this nonrelationship between men and women in the terms of Fregian functions in Seminars XIX . . . *ou pire* and XX *Encore*, in what he calls the "formulas of sexuation": $\forall x\ \Phi x$ / $\exists x\ \overline{\Phi x}$ and $\overline{\forall x}\ \Phi x$ / $\overline{\exists x}\ \overline{\Phi x}$. The first set of terms represents the logical structure of a man and the second set of terms represents the logical structure of a woman. The formulation $\forall x\ \Phi x$ signifies the universality of castration for men: the upside-down A is the universal quantifier "All" and the Φ is the phallic signifier, the mark of castration (as well as the residual phallic jouissance left over from castration), so we can read it as "all subjects who locate themselves as 'men' are subjected to the phallic function, castration." The last of the four formulations, $\overline{\exists x}\ \overline{\Phi x}$, represents the universality of castration for women (by means of the negation of the existential signifier, $\exists$), which we can thus read as "there is *no* subject that *is not* submitted to the phallic function."

14. The development of intuitionistic logic is attributed to Luitzen Egbertus Jan Brouwer; see his essay "Intuitionism and Formalism," trans. A. Dresden, *Bulletin of the American Mathematical Society*, 20 (1913); available electronically: http://www.ams.org/journals/bull/2000-37-01/

S0273–0979–99–00802–2/S0273–0979–99–00802–2.
pdf. Also see Arend Heyting, *Intuitionism: An Introduction*, 3rd rev. ed. (Amsterdam: North-Holland, 1971). It is
worth noting that Badiou has written a detailed analysis of
certain problems in Lacan's account of sexuation in "The
Subject and Infinity" (*Conditions,* trans. Steven Corcoran
[New York: Continuum, 2008]). Badiou points out that
whereas for Aristotle, the negation of the universal $\overline{\forall x}$
Φx, "not-all x is under the phallic function") is equivalent
to the affirmation of a particular ($\exists x\ \overline{\Phi x}$: "there is an x that
is not under the phallic function"), this is not the case in
Lacan's account of feminine sexuation. There cannot be a
particular woman who is not-all in the sense of being not
fully subject to the phallic function, since she would not be
able to speak (insofar as castration or the phallic function is
the condition of language). Badiou cites a passage from ...
ou pire and points out Lacan's apparent solution: "far from
indicating that it is possible to extract an affirmative from
it, such that 'one' exists who is not under the effect of castration, the *pas-toute*, on the contrary, points to a particular
mode of that effect, namely, that it is 'somewhere' and not
everywhere. The for-all (*pour-tout*) of the 'man' position is
also an 'everywhere.' The *somewhere, and not everywhere*, of
the 'woman' position is expressed: *pas-toute*" (215, emphasis
added). Yet in avoiding the problem of positing the existence
of a particular woman who is not-all, Lacan is forced to
pursue two mutually contradictory argumentative paths: the
assumption of an intuitionist logic (which would avoid the
implication from the negation of the universal to the affirmation of a particular) *and* the assumption of actual infinity,
which Lacan insists on in Seminar XX. As Badiou points
out, intuitionistic logic does not admit the actual existence

of infinite numbers, hence there is a serious contradiction in Lacan's attempt to suture logical intuitionism and the set theoretical idea of infinity.

15. This is expressed in the upper left side of the formulas of sexuation as $\exists x \overline{\Phi x}$, which we can read as "there is a subject who is not submitted to the phallic function." One way to understand this idea is in terms of the myth of the Father of the Primal Horde that Freud proposes (based on Darwin's speculations) in *Totem and Taboo*. In "L'Étourdit" Lacan discusses the relationship of this "saying no," the exception of the Primal Father, to psychosis, whose mechanism he elsewhere theorizes as a function of foreclosure (*forclusion*—his translation of Freud's term *Verwerfung*), the repudiation of "the Name-of-the-Father" [*le Nom-du-Père*] (AE 458).

16. Lacan writes, that insofar as the subject located as a woman "does not exist through a suspension of the phallic function," her "all" is "outside of the universe . . . as *notall*" [*n'existant pas de suspens à la fonction phallique . . . Mais c'est un tout d'hors univers . . . comme* pastout] (AE 466).

17. Each woman enters into her sexuality in a singular fashion, according to Lacan, who cites "the feminine myth of Don Juan," who, in Mozart's *Don Giovanni*, takes them "one by one," as they are recorded in Leporello's notebook: "If there are *mille e tre* of them, it's clear that one can take them one by one—that is what is essential. That is entirely different from the One of universal fusion. If woman were not not-all—if, in her body she were not not-all as sexed being—none of that would hold true." *The Seminar of Jacques Lacan. Book XX, Encore: On Feminine Sexuality, The Limits of Love and Knowledge, 1972–1973,* ed. Jacques-Alain Miller and trans. Bruce Fink (New York: Norton, 1998); p.10, translation very slightly modified).

18. *Encore*, 35. Cited by Cassin (23).

19. Jacques-Alain Miller devoted a year of his seminar (1983–84), entitled *Des réponses du Réel*, to the implications of this phrase.

20. *The Complete Works of Aristotle*, vol. 2, ed. by Jonathan Barnes (Princeton: Princeton University Press, 1984), 1588.

21. Cassin argues that Aristotle needs the Sophists as the exception that proves the rule of logic by constituting its outside, but avoids confronting this necessity: "When he formulated the universality of the principle of non-contradiction, Aristotle kept at bay the notion that the other was needed . . . that he needed the sophist as the basis for the principle." And for Cassin Lacan will take that role in modernity: "Lacan returns as a sophist, but a sophist who is defined as being necessary to Aristotle's principle, which is to say there is no universal proposition without an exception that founds it" (20).

22. See Adrian Johnston's very strong account of "ab-sense" in Badiou's reading of "L'Étourdit" in chapter 10, "Antiphilosophy and Paraphilosophy: Milner, Badiou, and Antiphilosophical Lacanianism" of *Adventures in Transcendental Materialism: Dialogues with Contemporary Thinkers* (Edinburgh: Edinburgh University Press, 2014).

23. Cassin points out and is apparently disappointed by the fact that, despite his critique of Aristotle's logic, Lacan uses the same taxonomy as Aristotle does (words, sentences, arguments) to distinguish modes of equivocation in "L'Étourdit."

24. See translators' note 5 on p. 74.

25. See translators' note 79 on p. 88.

26. Novalis, *Philosophical Writings,* ed. and trans. Margaret Mahony Stoljar (Albany: SUNY Press, 1997), 83. Kenneth

Burke also uses the term, apparently without reference to Novalis. See *The Rhetoric of Religion: Studies in Logology* (Oakland: University of California Press, 1970).

27. Cassin, *Jacques le sophiste,* 67.

28. See Aristotle, *Metaphysics* Book *Gamma*, 1009a, in *Complete Works of Aristotle,* 2:1593, ed. Jonathan Barnes, cited by Cassin, *Jacques le sophiste,* 67–68.

29. Lacan does not use the term *mathème*, as far as I can tell, until 1971 when it appears in the series of talks he gave at Sainte-Anne Hospital in parallel with his *Seminar XIX . . . ou pire,* which goes under the name *Le savoir du psychanalyste* (unpublished). Interestingly, in his apparent first coinage of the term on December 2, 1971, it is as something that holds the place of the variable, without for that simply manifesting the void, and embodies a certain truthfulness: "it is absolutely not true to talk about the matheme as something that is in any way detached from the requirement of truth" ("il n'est absolument pas vrai de parler du mathème comme de quelque chose qui d'aucune façon serait détaché de l'exigence véridique").

30. See Alain Badiou, *The Century,* ed. and trans. Alberto Toscano (Malden, MA: Polity, 2007), 146–47.

31. Recall too that in Freud's famous dream of Irma's Injection in *The Interpretation of Dreams,* "the chemical formula" of trimethylamin "printed in heavy type" appears to Freud as a revelation "of special importance," not only, as "one of the products of sexual metabolism," disclosing the meaning of the dream (and, as Freud's "specimen dream," the meaning of dreams more generally) as "sexuality," but sexuality *as a formula,* more "magic," however, than science: signified as *unknown.* As Lacan points out in his reading of this dream

in *Seminar II*, the "formula" revealed to Freud is like the "writing on the wall" inscribed by a disembodied hand in the Book of Daniel: however it may be interpreted, its signifies, first of all, its own facticity, its status as writing, and, second, "the very nature of the symbolic," symbolization as such. Freud, *Standard Edition* (4:116); Lacan, *Seminar II: The Ego in Freud's Theory and in the Technique of Psychoanalysis, 1954–1955*, trans. Sylvana Tomaselli (New York: Norton, 1991).

32. In his seminar on Lacan, Badiou deals at length with Lacan's claim that the project of psychoanalysis is to "raise impotence to the level of impossibility," a formulation that he describes as the most precious of all of Lacan's many "verbal treasures"—and perhaps even the best definition of philosophy itself (10). Lacan begins to develop the relationship between "impotence" and "impossibility" in *Seminar 17: The Other Side of Psychoanalysis,* trans. Russell Grigg (New York: Norton, 2007), and it remains key through at least *Seminar 22: R.S.I.* (unpublished).

AUTHORS' INTRODUCTION

1. Jacques Lacan, "L'Étourdit," *Scilicet* 4 (1973): 5–52; *Autres écrits* (Paris: Seuil, 2001: 449–95. All further page references will be to both the *Scilicet* and the *Autres écrits* edition, and will be indicated in parentheses herein, in that order.

Lacan's coinage *l'étourdit* is based on the French word *étourdi*, which means "scatterbrained" or "thoughtless"; Richard Wilbur translates the title of Molière's play *L'Étourdi* as *The Bungler*. The *t* at the end of *l'étourdit* is silent, but its addition suggests the French word *dit*, meaning "what is said," which Lacan distinguishes from *dire*, "the saying" or "the act of

saying." See Bruce Fink's excellent footnote on *l'étourdit* in his translation of Lacan's seminar *Encore* (note 5, p. 15, citation following).—Trans.

> 2. In English *Encore* was published as *The Seminar of Jacques
> Lacan. Book XX, Encore: On Feminine Sexuality, The Limits
> of Love and Knowledge, 1972–1973,* ed. Jacques-Alain Miller,
> trans. Bruce Fink (New York: Norton, 1998). All further
> references to *Encore* will be to this English-language edi-
> tion.—Trans.
>
> 3. The Belgian psychoanalyst, Christian Fierens, has devoted
> almost five hundred pages to "L'Étourdit" in two very help-
> ful books, *Lecture de l'Étourdit* (Paris: L'Harmatton, 2002)
> and *Le Discours psychanalytique: Une deuxième lecture de
> l'Étourdit de Lacan* (Toulouse: Érès, 2012).—Trans.
>
> 4. Lacan uses this coinage *fixion,* a condensation of *fiction*
> and *fix,* several times in "L'Étourdit," where it seems to
> refer to a fixing of the real in language, in which truth has
> the structure of a fiction. In Colette Soler's *Lacan— The
> Unconscious Reinvented,* trans. by Esther Faye and Susan
> Schwartz (London: Karnak, 2014), 131, she associates it
> with the symptom—Trans.

AB-SENSE, OR LACAN FROM A TO D

Full bibliographical references to those of Lacan's seminars that have been
published will be given when they first appear in the text; when English
translations of those seminars have been published, references will also
be given. References to Lacan's unpublished seminars will be indicated
by title and session date.

"HIHANAPPÂT": Although this term does not appear in the
published edition of . . . *ou pire* (ed. Jacques-Alain Miller [Paris: Seuil,
2011]), Lacan spells it out, as a homophonic version of *y en a pas* ("there

isn't any"): "It should be written as *hi! han!* [hee haw] and *appât* [bait, lure], with two *p*'s and a circumflex on the second *a* and a *t* at the end" (*OP* 27)—Trans.

1. Cassin's reference here is to a line from the French writer Henry de Montherlant's *Pitié pour les femmes* (1936), "La 'contre-nature' est la nature même, comme le contre-torpilleur est bel et bien un torpilleur"—Trans.

2. "Empirer," which Lacan puts in quotation marks here, is a pun on "empire" and the verb *empirer*, "to worsen," "to make worse;" it may also suggest *empyrée*, "empyrean," and the title of Lacan's seminar . . . *ou pire*—Trans.

3. Cassin will return to the "joke about the *mêden*" later in this essay, and at greater length in her recent book *Jacques le sophiste: Lacan, logos et psychanalyse* (Paris: EPEL, 2012), which expands on many of the ideas presented here—Trans.

4. "Strip" (*bande*) here probably refers to the Möbius strip (*bande de Moebius*), which Lacan had discussed earlier in this essay—Trans.

5. Lacan's phrase, "le passager clandestin dont le *clam* fait maintenant notre destin," plays on *clandestin*, breaking it into *clam* (the French root of the Medieval Latin for "secret," pronounced the same way as *clan*) and *destin*, "destiny." The phrase, moreover, seems to echo what he calls the "stowaway" (*passager clandestin*) function of *den* in the Greek word *mêden*—Trans.

6. Lacan's term here, *mots ravis*, may also be a pun on *Moravie*, or Moravia, where Freud was born—Trans.

7. Hyppolytus, *Refutations of All Heresies*, trans. F. Legge, 2 vols. (New York: MacMillan, 1921), 1:49. The Democritus fragment is DK 65 A40 in Hermann Diels and Walther Kranz, *Die Fragmente der Vorsokratiker*, 3 vols. (Zurich: Weidmann, 1969), 2:94.

See note 61, this chapter—Trans.

8. "Haven't you noticed that when people say that So-and-so is an idiot it actually means he's not so stupid [*un pas-si-con*]? What's depressing is that you don't know very well in what way he deals with jouissance. And that's why he is called an idiot." *The Seminar of Jacques Lacan: Book XVII: The Other Side of Psychoanalysis,* trans. Russell Grigg (New York: Norton, 2007), p. 71 (translation slightly modified).

9. Lacan points out that Michelet here is not the French historian but the nineteenth-century German philosopher Karl Ludwig Michelet—Trans.

10. Barbara Cassin and Michel Narcy, *La Décision du sens. Le livre Gamma de la Métaphysique d'Aristote* (Paris: Vrin, 1989). See the diagram on p. 137 of that work, obtained by overlaying "L'Étourdit" onto *Gamma*, which can serve as a guide for what follows.

11. Aristotle, *Metaphysics, Gamma* 3, 1005b 19–23, trans. W. D. Ross, in *The Complete Works of Aristotle: The Revised Oxford Translation,* ed. Jonathan Barnes, 2 vols. (Princeton: Princeton University Press, 1995), 2:1588. All further references to Book *Gamma* will be to this edition and will be indicated parenthetically in the text.

12. Cassin is quoting Lacan here: "read Aristotle's *Metaphysics,* and I hope you'll feel, as I do, that it's incredibly stupid [*vachement con*]" (*OP* 28)—Trans.

13. See Cassin and Narcy, *La Décision du sens*—Trans.

14. See Barbara Cassin, *Aristote et le logos. Contes de la phénoménologie ordinaire* (Paris: PUF, 1997), chapter 1.

15. One of the challenges for the translators of this text was the ubiquity of the French word *sens*, usually translated as "meaning" but often, in philosophical works in particular,

as "sense." Given the tremendous emphasis on Lacanian and other neologisms such as *ab-sens, sens ab-sexe, non-sens,* etc. in both Cassin's and Badiou's essays, we have opted for "sense" in most cases. It is hoped that the reader will have no difficulty tolerating this sort of "terminological dissonance," as Bruno Bosteels has called the dilemma in his "Translator's Preface" to Badiou's *Wittgenstein's Antiphilosophy*—Trans.

16. The distinction between *signification* and *sens* has historically been understood in various ways; frequently, *signification* refers to the relationship internal to a sign between a signifier and a signified, whereas *sens* (sense or meaning) refers to the representational function of a sign in a particular context of other signs—Trans.

17. Chapter 1 of [Aristotle's] *On Interpretation* establishes a sequence of "affections in the soul" (*ta en têi psukhêi pathê-mata*), "spoken sounds" (*ta en têi phônêi*) that are the symbols of them, and "written marks" (*ta graphomena*) that are in turn the symbols of spoken sounds. For a fuller interpretation of this sequence, which presents textual problems, see the entry "sign" in my *Dictionary of Untranslatables: A Philosophical Lexicon*, ed. Emily Apter, Jacques Lezra, and Michael Wood (Princeton: Princeton University Press, 2014), p. 976.

18. We are rendering Lacan's neologism *parest*, which condenses *paraît* (from *paraître*, "to appear" or "seem") and *est* (from *être*, "to be") as "sims," a condensation of "seems" and "is"—Trans.

19. As Anthony Chadwick notes in his translation of "L'Étourdit" (http://www.scribd.com/doc/56094420/Etourdit-Inte-grated), Lacan's term *dauphins* can mean both "dolphins" and "dauphins," the hereditary successors to the French throne, and by extension the next-in-line for the head of a major enterprise—Trans.

20. This line from "L'Étourdit" (5; 449) "Qu'on dise reste oublié derrière ce qui se dit dans ce qui s'entend" appears in *Encore* (p. 15) as well as in a slightly modified form in Seminar XIX (. . . *ou pire,* p. 221). The verb *s'entendre* can mean both "to be heard" and "to be understood." *Qu'on dise* is a subjunctive construction, allowing for it to be understood as meaning either "that one says" or "that one may say"—Trans.

21. In French, *les lettres* can also mean "literature"—Trans.

22. Jacques Lacan, "Conférences et entretiens dans des universités nord-américaines: Yale University, Kanzer Seminar, 24 novembre 1975," *Scilicet* 6/7 (1975): 35. These texts often strike me as being plainer, deciphered versions of that of which "L'Étourdit" is a performance, a speech act.

The French word translated here as "waves" is *vagues,* which is a pun on "vague" in the sense of indefinite or equivocal—Trans.

23. During the study day devoted to "L'Étourdit" that Alain Badiou and I organized at the École Normale Supérieure with Françoise Gorog and Diana Rabinovich, both of whom were our invaluable collaborators in every way, Elisabete Thamer undertook an exploration of the text's relationship to *On Sophistical Refutations.* I would like to express my appreciation to her here.

24. "Sarkozy m'à tuer" is an allusion to a notorious case in France in which a gardener, Omar Raddad, was accused of murdering his employer, Ghislaine Marchal, in 1991 on the basis of the grammatically incorrect sentence "Omar m'a tuer" (in proper French: "Omar m'a tuée") written in blood on a wall at the scene of the crime. Using a version of the instantly recognizable sentence as the title of an article she wrote (in *Le Monde,* February 28, 2009), "Sarkozy m'à

tuer," Cassin attacked the French president's utter disdain for culture, for language in particular, as evidenced in part by the numerous spelling mistakes on the official French government Web site during his term in office—Trans.

25. "Les poules couvent au couvent" ("Hens brood in the convent") demonstrates that homonyms (*couvent* = brood; convent) are not necessarily homophonic: the word is pronounced differently in this case depending on whether it is a verb or a noun. See the film *Amélie*, where the title character tries to read a similar phrase, meant to illustrate the complexities of French pronunciation: "Les poules couvent souvent au couvent" ("Hens often brood in the convent")—Trans.

26. See Barbara Cassin, *L'Effet sophistique* (Paris: Gallimard, 1995), pp. 353–57 in particular.

27. The Greek word *pharmakon* and its variants can mean both a "poison" and a "remedy"—Trans.

28. Molière, *The Bungler*, act 3, scene 1, l. 919, trans. Richard Wilbur (New York: Theatre Communications Group, 2010), p. 60.

29. Lacan uses the term *hontologie*, a portmanteau word combining *honte* ("shame") and *ontologie* ("ontology"), in the final session of his Seminar XVII, *The Other Side of Psychoanalysis* (p. 180)—Trans.

30. In this citation, the phrase "*du dit de chacun*" could also have been translated as "from what is said by each of them" or "from the said/statement/spoken of each of them." Similarly, "*les parties du discours*," which Lacan has put in quotation marks, we have rendered as "the parts of speech," although it might also have been translated as "parts of the discourse" or "parts of what they have said"—Trans.

31. See note 20—Trans.

32. *On Sophistical Refutations*, in particular chapters 20 and 21. Following the Stoics, Galen proposes a very fine homonymically divided homophony: *auletris peptoke* / *aule tris peptoke*: "the flutist fell" / "the courtyard collapsed three times in a row." See Barbara Cassin, "Des sophismes liés à l'expression" (1–4), in *L'Effet sophistique*, pp. 519–33.

33. Lacan's wordplay here is difficult to convey in English. It involves the contrast in French between the words *l'endroit* and *l'envers,* which can mean, variously, the wrong side and the right side, the front and the back, the face and the reverse, forwards and backwards, upside down and right side up, etc. To complicate matters, *à cet endroit* here means "in this respect," or, as we have translated it to retain at least part of the pun, "on this front." "From my opposite side" is meant to imply Lacan's oppositional stance, in this case, toward Freud, which he admits here—Trans.

34. Here Cassin is intentionally conflating the so-called Liar's Paradox (attributed to Epimenides of Crete, who is reputed to have said that all Cretans are liars) and the Jewish joke Freud cites in *Jokes and Their Relation to the Unconscious*: "Two Jews met in a railway carriage at a station in Galicia. 'Where are you going?' asked one. 'To Cracow,' was the answer. 'What a liar you are!' broke out the other. 'If you say you're going to Cracow, you want me to believe you're going to Lemberg. But I know in fact you're going to Cracow. So why are you lying to me?'" Sigmund Freud, *The Standard Edition of the Complete Psychological Works of Sigmund Freud,* ed. James Strachey (London: Hogarth, 1960), 8:115—Trans.

35. Book *Gamma* begins with *to on legetai pollakhos,* "being is said in various ways," and ends by giving way to Book *Delta,* which is no less than the first dictionary of philosophy.

36. The "gain in meaning" and coherence that makes the assump-

tion of the unconscious "necessary and legitimate" is designated as such in "The Unconscious," in Freud's *Papers on Metapsychology*. Lacan takes the opposite approach from Freud's in *Jokes and Their Relation to the Unconscious*. In his analysis of the salmon mayonnaise joke, Freud moves from nonsense posing as sense (see Sigmund Freud, *Le Mot d'esprit et sa relation à l'inconscient,* trans. Marie Bonaparte and M. Nathan [Paris: Gallimard, 1930], p. 79) to the sense in nonsense (p. 82)—i.e., the truth of the drive. In *Le Séminaire. Livre IV: La Relation d'objet* (Object relations), ed. Jacques-Alain Miller (Paris: Seuil, 1994), on the other hand, in order to comment on dreams and *Witz,* Lacan switches from the "new meaning" introduced by the existence of the signifier ("a different meaning," "a creation of meaning," p. 293) to the "fundamental nonsense of all use of sense" (p. 294). I have commented on this change in *L'Effet sophistique,* pp. 386–408.

37. See chapter 4, *"L'écrit et la vérité"* (Writing and truth), in *Le Séminaire. Livre XVIII: D'un discours qui ne serait pas du semblant* (On a discourse that would not be pure semblance), ed. Jacques-Alain Miller (Paris: Seuil, 2007), p. 73: "If you claim that one cannot at the same time say yes and no about the same point, there you win . . . but if you bet that it's either yes or no, there you lose." We can only know something about the truth "when it is unleashed," whence serious (i.e., not perverse) people's idea that the non-existence of the sexual relationship is "identical" to what is called freedom."

Paul Lorenzen (1915–1994) was a major German philosopher and mathematician—Trans.

38. . . . *ou pire* (session of January 12), on the other hand, with
its reference to the sophist, does designate the impasses
of logic as opening onto the Real, the sexual relationship
insofar as it cannot be written:

The Real establishes itself, by an effect that is by no means
the least important one, by establishing itself in the impasses
of logic. . . . Here, in a field that is seemingly the most certain
[arithmetic], we encounter something that's opposed to the
entire realm of discourse, to the exhaustion of logic, something that introduces an irreducible gap into it. That's where
I designate the Real. . . . It is the first stirrings (why not say as
much?) of the critique by which the sophist—to anyone who
states what is always posited as truth—by which the sophist
shows him that he doesn't know what he's saying. That is even
the origin of all dialectics.

Cassin's citation is from unpublished transcripts of Lacan's seminar; the
passage is slightly different in the only recently available published edition
of . . . *ou pire* (p. 41)—Trans.

39. *Le Séminaire. Livre XII: Problèmes cruciaux pour la psychanalyse*, session of May 12, 1965.

40. Jacques Lacan, "Conférences et entretiens dans des universités nord-américaines: Columbia University, Auditorium
School of International Affairs, 1er décembre 1975," *Scilicet*
6/7 (1975): 49.

41. *Le Savoir du psychanalyste* (The psychoanalyst's knowledge),
session of November 4, 1971.

42. Here is what comes just before this: "He [Freud] wasn't
doing science; he was creating a certain practice that could

be characterized as medicine's last flowering. This last flowering found refuge here [in France] because medicine had so
many ways of operating, completely mapped out in advance,
in a highly regulated way, that it was bound to come up
against the fact there were symptoms that had nothing to
do with the body but only with the fact that human beings
are afflicted, so to speak, with language." Lacan, "Kanzer
Seminar," p. 18.

43. In *Le Savoir du psychanalyste* (session of April 11, 1971) Lacan
comments on the old saying "the exception proves the rule"
in the context of a discussion of Aristotle—Trans.

44. "The fact that I state the existence of a subject by positing it
from a saying no to the propositional function Φx implies
that it is inscribed by a quantifier that this function is cut off
from because in this regard it can't be considered as truth,
which means as error either, the false to be understood only
as *falsus* in the sense of something fallen, a point I've already
stressed" ("L'Étourdit," pp. 15; 459).

45. "The best thing would be for me to make an effort and
show you how I write it: *dit-mension*" (Lacan, "Columbia
University," p. 42).

Lacan often writes the word "dimension" as the homophonic *dit-mension*,
which suggests two French words, *dit* ("what is said") and *mension*, which
he associates with *mensonge* (a "lie"): "*Dit-mension* is *mension* of the said.
This way of writing has an advantage, which is to allow *mension* to be
extended into *mensionge*, which indicates that what is said is not at all
necessarily true" (*Le Séminaire. Livre XXIII: Le sinthome* [The sinthome],
ed. Jacques-Alain Miller [Paris: Seuil, 2005], p. 144)—Trans.

46. Lacan, "Kanzer Seminar," p. 34.

47. Jacques Lacan, "Conférences et entretiens dans des universités américaines: Massachusetts Institute of Technology, 2 décembre 1975," *Scilicet* 6/7 (1975): 60.

48. "La Troisième" [The third], a paper delivered in Rome on November 1, 1974, at the Seventh Congress of L'École freudienne de Paris and subsequently published in *Lettres de l'École freudienne* 16 (1975): 177–203.

49. The translation of this line is from Bruce Fink's *Fundamentals of Psychoanalytic Technique: A Lacanian Approach for Practitioners* (New York: Norton, 2011), p. 29—Trans.

50. *OS*, session of June 17, 1970, p. 180.

51. "The fact that there's no such thing as a sexual relationship I've already established in this form, namely, that there's currently no way of writing it" (*D* 83).

52. In a remarkable footnote, the translator of *Encore,* Bruce Fink, explains several possible resonances in Lacan's coinage in this passage: *courcourant* (which doubles the first syllable of *courant* [current]) and its echo of his neologism two paragraphs earlier, *disque-ourcourant*, which sounds like *discours courant*, "the current discourse" and suggests the rotation of a phonograph record—Trans.

53. On the "as" see note 55, this chapter—Trans.

54. The allusion here is to J. L. Austin's classic work *How to Do Things with Words,* which Cassin previously discussed in an article entitled "Sophistics, Rhetorics and Performance; or How to Really Do Things with Words," in *Philosophy and Rhetoric* 42, no. 4 (2009): 349–72. Sophistics, she noted there, "is in a way the paradigm of discourse that does things with words" (p. 349)—Trans.

55. *Apophansis* means letting-be-seen; for Aristotle, an apophantic assertion or judgment directly *shows* something

about something, as opposed to comparative judgments. In *Being and Time*, Heidegger distinguishes the existential-hermeneutical "as" of ontology from the apophantical "as" of ontic statements: "The [apophantic] 'as' is forced back to the uniform level of what is merely objectively present. It dwindles to the structure of just letting what is objectively present be seen by way of determination. This levelling down of the primordial 'as' of circumspect interpretation to the as of the determination of objective presence is the speciality of the statement.... We call primordial the 'as' of circumspect interpretation that understands (*hermêneia*) the existential-*hermeneutical* 'as' in distinction from the *apophantical* 'as' of the statement." *Being and Time*, trans. Joan Stambaugh (Albany: SUNY Press, 1996), p. 148—Trans.

56. The first person to have drawn attention (my attention, at any rate) to *den* and the first to have interpreted atomism on the basis of this invention of Democritus's and against its Aristotelian rewriting was Heinz Wismann in his seminars and, for example, in "Atomos Idea," *Neue Hefte für Philosophie* 15/16 (1979): 34–52.

57. Chantraine then refers to A. C. Moorhouse's article, "ΔEN in Classical Greek," *Classical Quarterly* 12, no. 2 (1962): 235–38.

58. Our translation of the last part of this sentence admittedly pales somewhat in comparison with Cassin's colorful phrase *toutes sauf ma mère* (literally, "all except for my mother"). The popular expression she uses here is an abridged form of *toutes les femmes sont des putes sauf ma mere:* "all women are whores, except for my mother"—Trans.

59. He refers here to Manu Leumann, *Homerische Wörter* (Basel: Verlag Friedrich Reinhardt 1950), p. 108.

60. See the other long passage where he discusses it, in *The Four Fundamental Concepts of Psychoanalysis: The Seminar of Jacques Lacan, Book XI,* ed. Jacques-Alain Miller and trans. Alan Sheridan (New York: Norton, 1998), p. 64.

61. The first edition by Diels, with a translation of the Greek into German, came out in 1903; it was revised by Kranz in 1935 and has been reprinted in this same form many times up to this day (by Verlag Weidmann, Dublin and Zurich). The French translation (*Les Présocratiques*, ed. J.-P. Dumont, with the collaboration of D. Delattre and J.-L. Poirier [Paris: Gallimard, 1988]) is notoriously unreliable, and it is not always the difficulty of the texts that is solely to blame for this.

In English, see Kathleen Freeman, *Ancilla to the Pre-Socratic Philosophers: A Complete Translation of the Fragments in Diels, "Fragmente der Vorsokratiker"* (Cambridge: Harvard University Press, 1948)—Trans.

62. Plutarch, *Against Colotes,* in *Early Greek Philosophy,* trans. Jonathan Barnes (London: Penguin, 1988), p. 252 (translation modified to maintain consistency with the French text)—Trans.

63. The "pass" here refers to the Lacanian protocol for the end of analysis and the shift of the analysand into the position of analyst. The sequence of terms Cassin uses here (*la transmission, l'interprétation, la déformation, la réfection et le défaut—la passe*) all could refer to aspects of Lacanian psychoanalysis, as well as philology—Trans.

64. For a taste of this, see my article "Transmettre la philosophie grecque. Construire l'origine," *Cahiers de la Villa Gillet* 10 (1999): 123–35.

65. Galen, *On the Elements According to Hippocrates,* ed. and trans. Phillip de Lacey (Berlin: Akademie, 1996), 61 (trans-

lation modified to maintain consistency with the French text). The passage concerns the Democritus fragment DK 156B, located in testimonium DK 49B.

DK 68B9 in C. C. W. Taylor, *The Atomists: Leucippus and Democritus. Fragments, A Text and Translation with Commentary* (Toronto: University of Toronto Press, 1999)—Trans.

> 66. Ibid., p. 61 (translation modified to maintain consistency with the French text)—Trans.
> 67. DK A37.

Simplicius, *Commentary on Aristotle's* On the Heavens, in Barnes, *Early Greek Philosophy*, p. 247 (translation slightly modified)—Trans.

> 68. The difference between the two is presented in Parmenides' *Poem*. See, for example, my commentary *Parménide. Sur la nature ou sur l'étant: la langue de l'être?* (Paris: Seuil, 1998), pp. 200–11.
> 69. The fact that it is a compound negation has an impact on the syntax of the meaning: when a compound negation follows a simple negation, it isn't an affirmation; rather, it reinforces the negation.
> 70. In Plato's citation (at 237a, *The Sophist*) of the Parmenides fragment 7, from which we get our knowledge of this line, it is difficult to say for sure whether "things that are not" (or "non-beings") is the subject of an "is" or the predicate of being; to know whether we should understand "for never shall this prevail, that things that are not, are," or: "for never shall this prevail: being of non-beings." For a discussion of all the hypotheses about the line's construc-

tion and translation, see my commentary *Parménide: Sur la nature ou sur l'étant: La langue de l'être?*, in particular pp. 179–80.

71. Plato, *The Sophist*, pp. 237d–e, trans. Seth Benardete in *The Being of the Beautiful: Plato's* Theaetetus, Sophist, *and* Statesman (Chicago: University of Chicago Press, 1984), II.28–9 (translation slightly modified).

72. Homer, *Odyssée,* trans. Victor Bérard, 3 vols. (Paris: Les Belles Lettres, 1963), 2:44*n*2.

Victor Bérard was a French politician and classicist, well-known for his translation of the *Odyssey*—Trans.

73. *The Odyssey*, trans. Robert Fagles (New York: Penguin, 1996), pp. 222–23. (It's actually a Western.)

74. Translation modified by the author.

75. Édouard Pichon was a French linguist and psychoanalyst; with his uncle, Jacques Damourette, he was the author of a well-known French grammar, *Des mots à la pensée. Essai de Grammaire de la langue française*—Trans.

76. The reader may wish to consult Box 4 ("The French expletive *ne,* a vestige of *mê* ") in Cassin, *Dictionary of Untranslatables: A Philosophical Lexicon,* ed. Emily Apter, Jacques Lezra, and Michael Wood (Princeton: Princeton University Press, 2014), p. 321.

In French, the negative particle *ne* follows *personne* ("no one," "nobody") when *personne* is used as the subject of a verb in a negative sentence. Poly-phemus correctly omits the *ne* in his sentence ("C'est Personne qui me tue" or "Personne me tue," as Cassin conveys it a few lines before) because he is stating *affirmatively* that he is the victim of the man whose name is Personne. The other Cyclopes, however, hearing *personne*, assume the statement is *negative* and automatically add the *ne* where there is none: "Personne ne me tue" ("Nobody's killing me," meaning that Polyphemus is not being killed by anyone), thereby attributing their brother's trouble to the gods—Trans.

77. The word *mêtis* is certainly the master signifier of the episode, as witness its return, much later on, when Odysseus exhorts his heart to be patient: "Nobody but your cunning [*mêtis*] pulled you through the monster's cave you thought would be your death" (20.23–4). He'd had to add another ruse to his ruse, of course, and come up with the idea of getting out of the cave under the bellies of the sheep.

78. In French these negations are *pas* (step), *goutte* (drop), *mie* (crumb), and *que dalle* (uncertain origin, possibly from *le dail*, meaning "joke" or something whose meaning is hidden), respectively. As can easily be seen here in the first of these examples, English does not have an equivalent for *pas*, as the negation is conveyed by the simple placement of "do not/don't" before the verb—Trans.

79. We are translating Cassin's *ien* (which is *rien*, "nothing," with the first letter dropped) as "othing," and *iun* (a contraction of *ni un*, "not one," again with the first letter dropped) as "ot-one." In French, however, unlike English, *ien* and *iun* are homophonic and, incidentally, quite close to the Lacanian *hihanappât*. See Slavoj Žižek's commentary on Cassin's and Lacan's discussions of the *den* in *Less Than Nothing: Hegel and the Shadow of Dialectical Materialism* (New York: Verso, 2012), pp. 59–60—Trans.

80. "He did not say *hen*, let alone *on*. What, then, did he say? He said, answering the question I asked today, that of idealism, *Nothing, perhaps?*—not *perhaps nothing*, but *not nothing*"

(*The Four Fundamental Concepts of Psychoanalysis,* p. 64).
81. See note 2, this chapter—Trans.
82. In Seminar XIX, . . . *ou pire,* Lacan discusses Plato's account of "the one" in the *Parmenides* and coins the neologism *yad' lun,* which is a contraction of *il y a de l' Un,* which in English we could translate as "there is some One," or perhaps better, "there is something of One." The One, in Lacan's reading, is not originary, individual, or encompassing, but "the One of difference" (*OP* 191), the "one" that a set constitutes from multiple elements. Badiou begins his great work *Being and Event* with the decision that "the one *is not*"; however, "*there is,*" he writes, citing Lacan, "Oneness" (il y a *de l' Un*)—the one not as an ontological element but an *operation*: "In other words: there is no one, only the count-as-one." Alain Badiou, *Being and Event,* trans. Oliver Feltham (New York: Continuum, 2005), pp. 23–24—Trans.
83. Here is the entire passage from *The Four Fundamental Concepts of Psychoanalysis* that I've been commenting on in bits and pieces:

The *tuché* brings us back to the same point at which pre-Socratic philosophy sought to motivate the world itself. It required a *clinamen,* a swerve, at some point. When Democritus tried to designate it, presenting himself as already the adversary of a pure function of negativity in order to introduce thought into it, he says, *It is not the mêden that is essential,* and adds—thus showing you that from what one of my pupils called the archaic stage of philosophy, the manipulation of words was used, just as in the time of Heidegger—*it is not a* mêden *but a* den, which, in Greek, is a coined word. He did not say *hen,* let alone *on.* What, then, did he say? He said, answering the question I asked today, that of idealism, *Nothing, perhaps?*—not *perhaps nothing*, but *not nothing*.

(*The Four Fundamental Concepts of Pyschoanalysis*, 63–64 [translation slightly modified])

84. I've chosen this sophistic-atomistic-Lacanian-type phrase— "with the finest and most invisible body"– as the title for a collection of short stories that I would like to see act as philosophy's stowaway or, even better, as its *women* stowaways.

See Barbara Cassin, *Avec le plus petit et le plus inapparent des corps* (Paris: Fayard, 2007)—Trans.

85. Gorgias, *The Encomium of Helen*, in *The Greek Sophists*, ed. and trans. John Dillon and Tania Gergel (London: Penguin, 2003), p. 76, par. 8 (translation modified).

86. The homophonic play on the words *homme* and *(at)ome* in the French sentence—"Si le style, c'est l'homme, le tracé du stylet c'est l'atome"—can't be captured in English—Trans.

87. *Metaphysics* A, 985b 14–18. The comparison with letters is attested in the context of *On Generation and Corruption* as an example of the plasticity of the bonds between atoms: "For Tragedy and Comedy are both composed of *the same* letters" (I.2 315b 15).

88. *Stokheion*, according to Bruce Fink, means "element," "principal constituent," "letter," or "part of speech" (*E* 71*n*21)— Trans.

89. Jacques Lacan, *Le Séminaire. Livre IX: L'Identification,* sessions of November 29 and December 6, 1961.

90. The terms *l'être* and *lettre* are pronounced the same way in French—Trans.

91. Lacan's expression here, *même si je me tiens bien,* can also mean "even if I behave well"—Trans.

92. Alain Badiou, *Wittgenstein's Antiphilosophy,* trans. Bruno Bosteels (London: Verso, 2011), p. 146, quoting Lacan, *The Other Side of Psychoanalysis,* p. 61.

93. Cassin is quoting here from Badiou's essay in this volume "The Formulas of 'L'Étourdit'"—Trans.

94. Alain Badiou quotes this passage from "L'Étourdit" in his essay in this volume—Trans.

95. I'm paraphrasing Camille Morineau, the organizer of the remarkable exhibit "elles@centrepompidou": "The Museum is exhibiting only women, and yet the aim is neither to prove that women's art exists nor to produce a feminist project but for the public to regard this show as something like a beautiful history of twentieth-century art." *Elles@centrepompidou: Women Artists in the Collection of the Musée National d'Art Moderne* (Paris: Centre Pompidou, 2009), 16 (translation modified).

FORMULAS OF "L'ÉTOURDIT"

1. The line that Badiou paraphrases here is from Rimbaud's prose poem "Vagabonds": "moi, pressé de trouver le lieu et la formule" ("I, impatient to find the place and the formula"). Arthur Rimbaud, *Illuminations,* trans. Louise Varese (New York: New Directions, 1988), p. 64. Badiou discusses this line in *The Century,* p. 146—Trans.

2. Here we are translating *sens* as "meaning," but when it is in juxtaposition with *ab-sens* (as in the following paragraph) or otherwise indicated by context, we will translate it as "sense"—Trans.

3. Lacan writes in *Encore*: "Mathematical formalization is our goal, our ideal. Why? Because it alone is matheme, in other

words, it alone is capable of being integrally transmitted" (p. 119)—Trans.

4. Lacan discusses the relationship of "impotence" and "impossibility" in Seminar XVII, *The Other Side of Psychoanalysis*, especially in chapter 12, "The Impotence of Truth" (pp. 164–79). Badiou discusses the analytic process of elevating impotence to the level of logical impossibility in his seminar on Lacan. See *Le Séminaire. Lacan: L'antiphilosophie 3, 1994–1995* (Paris: Fayard, 2013). See especially the session of April 5, 1995 (pp. 191–210); forthcoming from Columba University Press as *The Seminar: Lacan, 1994–1995,* trans. Susan Spitzer, Kenneth Reinhard, and Jason Smith—Trans.

5. The verb *trancher* means to slice or cut off, but also has the sense of an act of "decision," a word that preserves some sense of its Latin root *caedere*, "to cut"—Trans.

6. Alain Badiou, *Wittgenstein's Antiphilosophy*, trans. Bruno Bosteels (London: Verso, 2011)—Trans.

7. By enclosing the word *savante* in quotation marks, Badiou alerts us to the double meaning, in this context, of the word, which denotes at once a relationship to knowledge and a respectful or deeply personal relationship. The latter sense in English seems to have disappeared largely from use except in a religious context (e.g., "a knowing relationship with God")—Trans.

8. The characters Monsieur and Madame Prudhomme, created by French playwright Henri Monnier in 1830, were the classic example of the nineteenth-century Parisian bourgeois couple. Joseph Prudhomme's speech was littered with fractured clichés like the one Badiou invents here: "robes . . . that fit me like a glove"—Trans.

9. The French term that Badiou uses here, *après-coup*, has special psychoanalytic meaning as Lacan's translation of Freud's term

nachträglich or, as a substantive, *Nachträglichkeit*, which is often translated as "deferred action" or "retroactive effect." See, e.g., *The Seminar of Jacques Lacan, Book II: The Ego in Freud's Theory and in the Technique of Psychoanalysis 1954–1955*, trans. Sylvana Tomaselli (New York: Norton, 1991), p. 185—Trans.

10. The French text reads: "qu'il y a eu *de* l'acte analytique" (our emphasis). This formulation using *de*—as opposed to the more straightforward "qu'il y a eu *un* acte analytique"—recalls Lacan's well-known dictum "*Y a* d'*l'un*" [our emphasis]. In a translator's note in *Encore* (p. 5), Bruce Fink suggest several different translations for this expression, including "There's something like One," which is the basis of our translation here—Trans.

11. In discussing the analytic act in the December 21, 1994, session of his seminar on Lacan, Badiou further elaborated: "It takes place in its own place, which is the couch (and/or the armchair?) and nothing more can be said about it. It can, however, be attested in the pass" Alain Badiou, *The Seminar: Lacan, 1994–1995,* trans. Susan Spitzer, Kenneth Reinhard, and Jason Smith (New York: Columba University Press, forthcoming)—Trans.

12. Badiou uses various versions of this term (*horlieu, hors-lieu*, and *hors de lieu*) in his book *Theory of the Subject*, where they imply not so much a place outside as a *place outside of place*—Trans.

13. Since English, unlike French, makes no distinction between the kinds of knowledge at stake in this essay, particularly in this paragraph and the next two, Adrian Johnston's helpful explanation is worth citing: "It is crucial to appreciate here the difference between knowing/ knowledge involving conscious acquaintance or familiarity (*connaître/connaissance*)

versus knowing/knowledge (*savoir*) as entailing conceptual, intellectual comprehension ... The truths of the unconscious, situated in the register of the Real, defy *connaissance* but not (analytic) *savoir*." *Adventures in Transcendental Materialism* (Edinburgh: Edinburgh University Press, 2014), p. 260—Trans.

14. In *Le séminaire, livre XIX . . . ou pire,* ed. Jacques-Alain Miller (Paris: Seuil, 2011), Lacan comments, "what allows us to escape from [fantasmatic reality] is, in the symbolic formula that we are able to extract from it, an impossibility that demonstrates its real [*en démontre le réel*]" (pp. 173–74)—Trans.

15. Badiou's expression here, *répondre à sa place*, can also mean "answer for itself" or "on its own behalf"—Trans.

16. Lacan discusses this concept extensively in Seminar X: Anxiety; see especially p. 297, where this quote is found. *The Seminar of Jacques Lacan, Book X: Anxiety,* ed. Jacques-Alain Miller and trans. A. R. Price (Malden, MA: Polity, 2014). Badiou devotes most of Session 7 (April 5, 1995) of his seminar on Lacan to anxiety. See Alain Badiou, *The Seminar: Lacan, 1994–1995*—Trans.

17. See Badiou's discussion of Lacan's essay "Logical Time and the Assertion of Anticipated Certainty: A New Sophism" in *Theory of the Subject,* trans. Bruno Bosteels (London: Continuum, 2009), 248–53. See also Alain Badiou, *The Seminar: Lacan, 1994–95*, in particular Session 7 (April 5, 1995)—Trans.

18. There is an untranslatable pun here, which Badiou calls attention to in the French text, involving the word *cure*. So far in this essay he has been using the word in its common acceptation to mean the analytic treatment. But here he

plays on another meaning of the word when he writes that, with regard to the external decision he has been discussing, philosophy *n'a cure* ("couldn't care less"). *Cure* once meant "care, worry, concern"; it survives in French today only in the negative expression *n'avoir cure de*—Trans.

19. Badiou's use of the expression "an un-known truth" (*une vérité in-sue*) echoes Lacan's expression in *Le savoir du psychanalyste* (lectures delivered at Sainte-Anne Hospital in tandem with Seminar XIX), where he refers to the "un-known knowledge" (*savoir in-su*) of the unconscious. Unpublished, session of November 4, 1971—Trans.

Index

Univocity, 47–62; of being, xxiii, 46; of sense, 8, 9
Un-sense, 9
Untranslatables, 21–22

"Vagabonds," xxiv–xxv, 91*n*1
Vagues. See Waves
Violence, 30–34
Void (*Mêden*), xx–xxi

Waves (*Vagues*), 77*n*22
Whores, 84*n*58
Wilbur, Richard, x, 72*n*1
Wismann, Heinz, 36, 37, 84*n*56

Wittgenstein's Antiphilosophy (Badiou), 48, 75*n*15
Woman-philosopher, 41–42
Women, xii–xvi, 23–24, 41–42, 67*n*13, 69*nn*16–17, 91*n*95; jouissance modes available to, 66*n*12; stowaways, 90*n*84; as whores, 84*n*58
Word, 21, 26, 41. *See also* Nothing
World (*L'univers*), 4
Writing, xv–xvi, 19, 23–24, 36–39, 71*n*31, 83*n*51
Writing and Truth (Lacan). *See L'Écrit et la vérité*

Insurrections:

CRITICAL STUDIES IN RELIGION, POLITICS, AND CULTURE

Slavoj Žižek, Clayton Crockett, Creston Davis, Jeffrey W. Robbins, Editors

Religion and the Specter of the West: Sikhism, India, Postcoloniality,
and the Politics of Translation,
Arvind Mandair
Plasticity at the Dusk of Writing: Dialectic, Destruction,
Deconstruction,
Catherine Malabou
Anatheism: Returning to God After God,
Richard Kearney
Rage and Time: A Psychopolitical Investigation,
Peter Sloterdijk
Radical Political Theology: Religion and Politics After Liberalism,
Clayton Crockett
Radical Democracy and Political Theology,
Jeffrey W. Robbins
Hegel and the Infinite: Religion, Politics, and Dialectic,
edited by Slavoj Žižek, Clayton Crockett, and Creston Davis
What Does a Jew Want? On Binationalism and Other Specters,
Udi Aloni
A Radical Philosophy of Saint Paul,
Stanislas Breton,
edited by Ward Blanton, translated by Joseph N. Ballan
Hermeneutic Communism: From Heidegger to Marx,
Gianni Vattimo and Santiago Zabala
Deleuze Beyond Badiou: Ontology, Multiplicity, and Event,
Clayton Crockett
Self and Emotional Life: Philosophy, Psychoanalysis, and
Neuroscience,
Adrian Johnston and Catherine Malabou
The Incident at Antioch: A Tragedy in Three Acts / L'Incident
d'Antioche: Tragédie en trois actes, *Alain Badiou,*
translated by Susan Spitzer

Philosophical Temperaments: From Plato to Foucault,
    Peter Sloterdijk

To Carl Schmitt: Letters and Reflections,
    Jacob Taubes,
    translated by Keith Tribe

Encountering Religion: Responsibility and Criticism After Secularism,
    Tyler Roberts

Spinoza for Our Time: Politics and Postmodernity,
    Antonio Negri,
    translated by William McCuaig

Factory of Strategy: Thirty-three Lessons on Lenin,
    Antonio Negri,
    translated by Arianna Bove

Cut of the Real: Subjectivity in Poststructuralism Philosophy,
    Katerina Kolozova

A Materialism for the Masses: Saint Paul and the Philosophy of
    Undying Life, *Ward Blanton*

Our Broad Present: Time and Contemporary Culture,
    Hans Ulrich Gumbrecht

Wrestling with the Angel: Experiments in Symbolic Life,
    Tracy McNulty

Cloud of the Impossible: Negative Theology and
    Planetary Entanglements,
    Catherine Keller

What Does Europe Want? The Union and Its Discontents,
    Slavoj Žižek and Srećko Horvat

Nietzsche Versus Paul,
    Abed Azzam

Paul's Summons to Messianic Life: Political Theology and
    the Coming Awakening,
    L. L. Welborn

Reimagining the Sacred: Richard Kearney Debates God with James
Wood, Catherine Keller, Charles Taylor, Julia Kristeva, Gianni
Vattimo, Simon Critchley, Jean-Luc Marion, John Caputo, David Tracy, Jens Zimmermann, and Merold Westphal,
edited by Richard Kearney and Jens Zimmermann

An Insurrectionist Manifesto: Four New Gospels for a Radical Politics,
Ward Blanton, Clayton Crockett, Jeffrey W. Robbins,
and Noëlle Vahanian

The Intimate Universal: The Hidden Porosity Among Religion, Art,
Philosophy, and Politics, *William Desmond*

Heidegger: His Life and His Philosophy, *Alain Badiou and Barbara*
Cassin, translated by Susan Spitzer

Sociophobia: Political Change in the Digital Utopia, *César Rendueles,*
translated by Heather Cleary

The Work of Art: Rethinking the Elementary Forms of Religious Life,
Michael Jackson